The old ones were efficient. They followed the stars, nature's ̲ ̲ ̲ ̲ ̲ ̲ messages of gods. They could embrace three virtues in a single gesture, binding together what was natural, practical, and mystical. More normal in our world is to separate these things, creating a different kind of efficiency, the efficiency of machines. Though we are busy and fast, our streets show plenty of rage and sorrow. Clearly there is something in us that remains unsatisfied. It stirs in our deeper natures, seeking to weave spirit, earth, and practical life together again. Cooking by moonlight is a wonderful way to begin.

—Dana Gerhardt

By inviting the moon to light our way and guide our steps, we open ourselves to the subtle rhythms of the natural world, and honor the tug of intuition within our bodies. We reawaken powerful goddess energy and bring enchantment back into our everyday life. We all have to eat. Why not make meals magical?

About the Author

Karri Ann Allrich is an author, artist, and magical cook. Her Scottish/Irish heritage infuses her with a love of all things Celtic. Inspired by the archetypal goddess, faery, and selkie lore, Karri Ann crafts her solitary hedge path by the sea. She shares her home and art studio with husband Steve Allrich, an author and artist, and their two strapping sons.

To Write to the Author

If you wish to contact the author or would like more information about this book, please write to the author in care of Llewellyn Worldwide and we will forward your request. Both the author and publisher appreciate hearing from you and learning of your enjoyment of this book and how it has helped you. Llewellyn Worldwide cannot guarantee that every letter written to the author can be answered, but all will be forwarded. Please write to:

Karri Ann Allrich
℅ Llewellyn Worldwide
P.O. Box 64383, Dept. 1-56718-015-9
St. Paul, MN 55164-0383, U.S.A.
Please enclose a self-addressed stamped envelope for reply,
or $1.00 to cover costs. If outside U.S.A., enclose
international postal reply coupon.

Many of Llewellyn's authors have websites with additional information and resources. For more information, please visit our website at http://www.llewellyn.com.

COOKING BY MOONLIGHT

A Witch's Guide to Culinary Magic

Karri Ann Allrich

2004
Llewellyn Publications
St. Paul, Minnesota 55164-0383, U.S.A.

FIRST EDITION
Second Printing, 2004

Book design by Donna Burch
Cover photo © 2003 by Leo Tushaus
Cover design by Gavin Dayton Duffy
Editing by Karin Simoneau
Interior illustration by Kevin R. Brown

Library of Congress Cataloging-in-Publication Data
Allrich, Karri.
  Cooking by moonlight : a witch's guide to culinary magic / Karri Ann Allrich ;
foreword by Dana Gerhardt.
    p. cm.
  Includes index.
  ISBN 1-56718-015-9
  1. Cookery. I. Title.

TX714 .A456 2002
641.5—dc21   2002034211

Llewellyn Worldwide does not participate in, endorse, or have any authority or responsibility concerning private business transactions between our authors and the public.

   All mail addressed to the author is forwarded but the publisher cannot, unless specifically instructed by the author, give out an address or phone number.

   Any Internet references contained in this work are current at publication time, but the publisher cannot guarantee that a specific location will continue to be maintained. Please refer to the publisher's website for links to authors' websites and other sources.

Llewellyn Publications
A Division of Llewellyn Worldwide, Ltd.
P.O. Box 64383, Dept. 1-56718-015-9
St. Paul, MN 55164-0383, U.S.A.
www.llewellyn.com

 Printed on recycled paper in the United States of America

For my husband, Steve,
and my sons,
Colin and Alex,
who walk in moonlit beauty.

Contents

Side Dishes and Vegetables   147

Sensuous Salads   173

Sweet Endings   183

Acknowledgments

Cooking By Moonlight originated in the hearth and heart of my home: around the wooden kitchen table scuffed and burnished by countless shared meals, Sunday newspapers, spilled coffee and bread flour. I owe immeasurable thanks and gratitude to my husband, Steve, and our sons, Colin and Alex, who willingly taste tested and critiqued recipes, offering up not only their taste buds but their keen emotional support. Appreciation goes out to my mother, Dorothy, who offered to kitchen test dessert recipes, bearing various samples of cake, tea bread, and pie to her weekly circle of knitters. Thank you, ladies! Thanks to my father, Alan, for the roasted vegetable chowder idea. And heartfelt gratitude to my mother-in-law, Lynn, who bought me a beautiful new stove when our old one ceased to function.

Thanks to all the divine women at Llewellyn, goddesses in their own right: Sandra Weschcke, Nancy Mostad, Lisa Braun, Natalie Harter, Donna Burch, Ann Kerns, and Sharon Leah. Special acknowledgment goes to my editor, Karin Simoneau, whose clarity and prudence shelters my words.

Personal thanks to Katya Petriwsky, Dana Gerhardt, Margie Lapanja, Pat Monaghan, Terence Winch, Ray Buckland, Raven Grimassi, Dorothy Morrison, Gillian Drake, Joan Graham, Karen North Wells, Dana Bennett, and Zanna at Infinity.

Heartfelt gratitude to fellow author and moon lover Elen Hawke, whose support, keen perception, and humor brighten my life.

FOREWORD

Keeping Aldebaran in Mind

Imagine you did not learn the months of the year in kindergarten. Imagine instead your mother and father watched the sky, waiting for the morning star Aldebaran to rise, and when it did, you knew you would finally get your bicycle. One lunar month later, when the morning star Rigel made its first appearance of the year, your mother would gather those sweet berries and bake them into a pie. High summer, you stayed up late, watching the moon grow bigger, brightening all the rooftops in your neighborhood. You grew sad as she waned to a morning crescent, knowing Sirius would soon appear, and school would begin again.

All grown up, you watch the skies now as your parents did, waiting each year for Aldebaran, loving how it ushers in an abundance of watermelon and strawberries at the grocery store. You keep an eye on the moon moving through her cycle and make a promise to yourself. Fasting on watermelon juice for the three days of the dark moon, you're flush with new energy when Rigel appears. Of course you wouldn't think of going a single day or night without looking skyward.

Imagine: friendlier than the clock, more familiar than the local weatherman, more dear than your new DVD player—the stars. Honoring your life as you honor them. In your house and every other house in your neighborhood, there's a row of eastern-facing windows. And in the farthest one, in your daughter's bedroom, Sirius will appear one late-summer morning, announcing that it's time to shop for a new backpack and new school clothes.

Of course, in real life, we don't need to look up. I think of explaining this to an ancestor, one who must have visited the natural calendar as regularly as I do television and the local gas station. "O ancestor, I need neither the seasons nor the moon. I do not change my work nor vary my meals with the sun. I travel in one day by car as far as you traveled in three moons by foot. I have a house big enough to shelter a small village, though there are only three of us. And we are as warm in winter as our energy bill is high."

"No sun, no moon, no stars?" There is a look of confusion on my ancestor's face, a sea of thoughts that churn until out comes a single question: "But then, who do you pray to?"

The old ones were efficient. They followed the stars, nature's supply of food, the whispered messages of gods. They could embrace three virtues in a single gesture, binding together what was natural, practical, and mystical. More normal in our world is to separate these things, creating a different kind of efficiency, the efficiency of machines. Though we are busy and fast, our streets show plenty of rage and sorrow. Clearly there is something in us that remains unsatisfied. It stirs in our deeper natures, seeking to weave spirit, earth, and practical life together again. Cooking by moonlight is a wonderful way to begin.

We can't (and shouldn't) recreate our ancestors' lives. Yet we still have the cycling moon that meant so much to them, the earth that offers up her bounty, and our lusty appetites. We have kitchens, grocery stores, and farmers' markets, plus family and friends to cook for. With the changing sky above, we have all that we need to make our own lives spirited, sensuous, and soulful. We are further blessed to have Karri Ann's guidance, taking us to body, intuition, and the Goddess' culinary skill.

—Dana Gerhardt

PREFACE

Culinary Magic by Moonlight

Each new moon offers us a spiritual lesson. Every full moon celebrates the lesson's fruition. Working with the moon and her phases has taught me many things. The subtle distinctions of each lunar cycle have trained me to listen, observe, and surrender. Honoring our intuition begins with simple things: deciding which foods to eat, when to rest, where to direct our focus, how to materialize our energy. Honoring our body and our intuition honors the essence of the Goddess.

Using the moon's seasonal lessons in the kitchen is as natural a match as honey and lemon. All women are born with natural instinct. All wise women feel an affinity with the moon. With moonlight guiding our path, we cultivate our deeper intuition and celebrate the seasons directly with our body, mind, and spirit . . . right in our own humble kitchen. Food becomes more than just fuel. Meals become magical. Magic becomes practical.

Becoming seasonally attuned and using your culinary skills in harmony with the moon is a direct and lovely way to cultivate enchantment in everyday life. The only magical tools you'll need are a favorite wooden spoon, an open mind, and a generous heart. So join me in cooking by moonlight, and stir up a little magic in your life!

INTRODUCTION

Seasonal Lessons

My first cookbook, *Cooking by the Seasons*, initiated me into exploring the concept of seasonal eating, finding valuable lessons from the Goddess tucked within her four seasons. From the cyclic Wheel of the Year, each turn marks a guise of the Great Mother Earth, each change brings its own distinct aromas, tastes, and colors into the kitchen.

By consciously setting aside time to mark this Wheel with celebration and tuning in to the wisdom of seasonal foods, we deepen our connection to nature's lessons; we create meals that are not only healthful, but sacred as well—food that nourishes both body and soul.

In *Cooking by Moonlight*, I dip into this notion even further. As a lover of the moon and her ever-changing influence, I began to tune in to the subtle changes of each month in the lunar year and explore the joys of ritual cooking. Every new moon brings a fresh lesson to be savored, each full moon blooms its potential. Modest changes from one lunar cycle to the next call for different food choices and distinct tastes. The perfect pumpkin soup recipe for October's moon of the falling leaves, spiked with warming spices to fortify body and spirit, is not quite fitting for the expansive blossoming energy of May's flower moon. Her seductive enchantment whispers the promise of love, and demands instead a light, fresh soup, the color of Aphrodite's favored tomatoes, laced with freshly picked mint. Observing and honoring these distinct lunar energies led me to this project, inspiring me to cook by moonlight.

Honoring Our Intuition Honors the Moon

As we explore the influence of the waxing and waning moons, learning to develop our intuition and tune in to the changing needs of our bodies throughout the turning of the year, we will focus our intention on simple ritual cooking and creating culinary alchemy, all the while immersing ourselves in the pleasures each season has to offer.

From the soul-satisfying comfort of grounding foods during the cold moons of winter to the lighter, newly picked bounty of a summer's garden under a sultry summer crescent, we will conjure up edible pleasures for every turn of the Goddess' guise. We will take delight in natural fresh flavors, herbs, and exotic spices, and revel in her tantalizing array of fragrant fruits and agricultural abundance.

For those omnivores among us, I have included recipes containing the Goddess' salt-kissed gifts from the sea (crab and fish), and fortifying dishes with chicken, turkey, and the simple but versatile egg. For vegetarians, nearly all main dish recipes are supplemented with a vegetarian version under "Moonlit Kitchen Tips," with simple substitutions provided. Each new moon's astrological lesson will be presented from an intuitive goddess viewpoint, along with a menu befitting that lunar month.

> *From the eternal dance of the seasons*
> *through each waxing and waning moon,*
> *to follow the Goddess is to walk*
> *the path of the sensual*
> *as well as the spiritual . . .*
> *for the body and the soul are one*
> *and both must be considered when*
> *thinking about nourishment.*

If we align ourselves with our intuition, encountering the world with our bodies as well as our minds, we will find that when it comes to food, that which feeds the body also feeds the soul. Magic happens! This is the essence of cooking by moonlight.

BY THE LIGHT OF THE MOON

Tuning in to the Moon's Cycles: Ritual Cooking

Each night in the dark sky above, we are witness to an ever-changing display, a starlit allegory reflecting simple truths about our human nature, our journey, our purpose. The moon becomes the symbol of the Goddess; her waxing and waning phases become a meditation on the cycle of growth, fruition, decline, and renewal. She is the archetypal Triple Goddess: Maiden, Mother, and Crone.

As we open ourselves to the Goddess, nature's expression of the feminine, we embrace her energy and allow her lunar lessons to guide us. Tuning in to her cycles of growth, ripening, decline, and rebirth, we are able to follow her ideal and bring her wisdom and magic into our hearts, our minds . . . and our kitchens. Our stove becomes the hub of our alchemy.

By using conscious intention and appropriate foods, herbs, and spices, we are able to import the sacred feminine into our daily routine. Ritual cooking does not have to be an elaborate enterprise with pomp and circumstance. In fact, I feel that its power stems from its very simplicity: the intimate, private experience with tools as simple as your favorite wooden spoon. Stirred with intentions of love, seduction, healing, health, or prosperity, daily meals can become the most powerful form of magic, holistically engaging our heart, mind, body, and spirit, creating culinary alchemy with every stir and morsel.

By inviting the moon to light our way and guide our steps, we open ourselves to the subtle rhythms of our natural world and honor the tug of intuition that sleeps softly within our bodies. We reawaken powerful goddess energy and bring enchantment back into our everyday life. We all have to eat. Why not make meals magical?

The Waxing Moon

The lesson of the crescent moon reflects the Goddess in her maiden aspect, full of promise and potential. This moon phase brings growth and renewal. It is a time for strengthening, energizing, and supporting creativity. As goddesses in the kitchen, this is the perfect time to try new recipes, experiment, stock our pantries, and expand our cooking skills.

When planning meals during the waxing moon, choose foods that build up strength, invigorate the mind, and revitalize body and soul. In working with magical intentions, set goals and visualize dreams coming true. Let your cooking conjure abundance, creativity, healing, and true love. Stir sauces and soups deosil (clockwise) with purpose, using appropriate herbs and spices to enhance your intention.

Kitchen Blessing for the Waxing Moon

Brigid, Goddess of the hearth and fire
ignite our hearts with your poetic spirit,
bright as flame—courageous, bountiful and true.
Keep abundant our pantry, our friends and our generosity.
Bless our table always with gentle nourishment and a welcoming chair.
Sanctify this home with peace and safety.
Watch over this kitchen so that it may always be rich in love and laughter. Blessed Be!

During the waxing phase of the moon, select natural tonics that stimulate the body and foods that build up strength.

Recipes calling for fish, chicken, meat, beans, grains, or yogurt are all strengthening. Build a meal around a pasta smothered with roasted vegetables, olive oil, and freshly shaved Parmesan cheese. Experiment with new flavors and try a new recipe that features spices you don't ordinarily use.

Vegetables such as broccoli, carrots, corn, and sweet potatoes are chock-full of immune-boosting vitamins. Choose a variety of vegetables in every color, and use them in soups and stews, roasted dinners and stir-fries.

Sweets such as puddings, ice creams, and yogurt smoothies are calorie and calcium rich. In warm weather try a new sorbet and serve it with your favorite cookie. In colder moons bake warm fruit crisps and cobblers with cinnamon and nutmeg.

Garlic and onion add the fire element to your cooking. Herbs like basil, fennel, and thyme energize the system and awaken the taste buds. Spices such as ginger, turmeric, and curry act as tonics and stimulate digestion. Make a spicy tea with slices of fresh ginger and a dab of local honey.

The Full Moon

The luminous round moon in all its fullness inspires lovers and poets, and, some say, the wild and crazy (hence the name "lunatic"). For those following the path of the Goddess, however, it is a sacred time, full of energy and magic, worship and celebration. Foods at this phase of the Goddess in her Mother aspect—weighty, and at her full potential—should be rich, abundant, and celebratory. This is the perfect time for culinary alchemy, as magical energies are intoxicating and expansive. Gather herbs from your garden in the early light of dawn, and visualize your dream, knowing it will be. Trust in the Mother to honor your desires.

Kitchen Blessing for the Full Moon
Goddess, Mother, the end and the beginning,
the dusk and the dawn, we celebrate you!
Bless us tonight as we gather in love,
watch over us with compassion,
and fill us with your grace.
Accept our thanksgiving as we lift up
our hearts in joy! Blessed Be!

During the full moon, celebrate!

A roasted turkey, baked salmon, egg dishes, and bowls of steaming pasta topped with garlicky shrimp or roasted vegetables and pine nuts are all perfect choices to revel in the full moon's energy. Choose foods for love that are sumptuous and seductive, and spices that are warm and sensuous.

Moon vegetables such as mushrooms, potatoes, cabbage, and snowy cauliflower should be prepared with creamy sauces spiked with caraway, or tarragon, or paired with basil and juicy tomatoes, the *fruit of love.*

Herbs and spices should be lively and uplifting, including mints, thyme, basil, and oregano. Use lots of freshly cracked peppercorns to add passion or protective energies. Spices should be fiery, like chili peppers and garlic, or sweet and alluring, like cinnamon and vanilla.

For a full moon dessert, celebrate sensuality goddess-style: eat from plates brimming over with ripened fruits in season, assorted nuts and cheeses, sweet wine . . . and anything chocolate!

The Waning Moon

The waning moon brings a turn toward introspection, finalizing details and clearing out that which we have outgrown or no longer need. It is a time to garner wisdom in the quiet, a time to let go. As the Goddess in her Crone aspect, this phase of the moon teaches patience and the development of inner wisdom—paying attention to intuition.

In the kitchen, we are clearing out, paring down, and finishing up leftovers. Take time to contemplate letting go of what no longer nourishes you in your life. Rid the refrigerator of stale and moldy foods with clear intention. As you discard the old, focus your thoughts on visualizing those aspects in your life that need to be cast off. My friend Dana disposes of her smelly kitchen sponge just before each new moon with such a purpose in mind. Consider that if there is no room in your cluttered refrigerator, or your life, there is no space for the new and marvelous to enter.

Kitchen Blessing for the Waning Moon

Cerridwen, Goddess of transformation,
inspire us with your bittersweet beauty
to be fierce in our clarity.
Help us to discard that which no longer nourishes us,
body and soul.
Keep our hearth free of clutter and lingering bones of contention.
Help us to stir our ancient dreams into reality.
Teach us to trust our instincts and honor our intuition.
Bless our path as we dedicate our home to the service of truth. Blessed Be!

During the waning moon, choose foods that cleanse the system and fortify protection.

Waning moon foods that help clear the body and cleanse accumulated energy include lemon and grapefruit, cabbage, celery, broccoli, cranberries, barley, parsley, sage, and bitter greens. Take the time during this waning moon to tune in to what your body is craving, and contemplate why you have these cravings. Pay close attention to your body's symptoms. Our bodies are a physical map of our unconscious, or unknown self.

Choose lighter proteins as the center of your meal, such as tofu, light fish, or yogurt. Beans are astringent, and served with brown rice they provide the perfect protein at this time of retreat. Experiment with simple meals based around beans, rice, and pungent spices.

Broth-based soups full of simmering vegetables, and light pastas such as angel hair tossed in olive oil, lemon, and garlic make a good choice for entrees during the waning phase. For another appropriate light meal, try some balsamic roasted vegetables served on slices of toasted French bread spread with fresh chèvre (goat cheese), and a fresh salad of herbal greens. Think light and fresh, clear and uncomplicated.

Cleansing and purifying herbs such as cilantro and parsley may be added to soups and salads, and sprinkled on vegetables. Add protective rosemary to your breads, biscuits, and roasted vegetables. Try a cucumber salad with a yogurt-dill dressing. Naturally sweet desserts such as apples, strawberries, or chilled watermelon are all astringent and cleansing choices.

Herbal teas are especially useful during the waning moon. Sage tea, the perfect Crone's tea, is antibiotic, and preventative as well as protective. Peppermint calms and soothes the tummy. Hot water with lemon helps cleanse the liver of excess energy. A tonic of warm water with a tablespoon of apple cider vinegar and local honey will boost your immune system and clear away impurities.

The New Moon

Also known as the dark moon, this three-day period brings us in touch with the depth of night and summons us to face the Dark Goddess energies. It is a powerful time of intention setting and soul searching. Many practitioners advise some form of fasting during the dark moon phase to aid in clearing the mind and body.

If you choose to fast, do so wisely and drink plenty of fluids, particularly supportive herb teas and freshly squeezed juices. As you begin eating again, choose simple nourishing foods to break your fast, such as yogurt with a piece of fruit. Savor each bite. You will feel as if your inner fire has been reset, and your body will welcome the coming waxing energy of the moon goddess with anticipation and delight. It's a wonderful way to break old habits and unconscious eating patterns. Tune in to making food choices consciously. This honors your body and, in turn, the goddess within.

New Moon Kitchen Blessing

Hecate, Goddess of the dark moon crossroads,
stay with us tonight. Be our silent witness.
Confirm our sorrow, loss and pain
with your unwavering strength and steady gaze.
Bless us with your hard won wisdom.
Guide us in new directions
as we let go of the past and embrace
our future. Blessed Be!

DEVELOPING SEASONAL INTUITION

As well as tuning our bodies in to the changing phases of the monthly moon, it is important to develop our seasonal intuition and learn the wisdom inherent in seasonal foods. Even though I thoroughly enjoy the new availability of balsamic vinegar and organic produce at the corner supermarket, the allure of imported strawberries in mid-January escapes me. I walk right past them without desire. In the midst of a wintry gray cold front, I crave the consolation of a cinnamon apple cake, or warmed sliced pears in brandy and brown sugar. My body needs comfort, not cooling.

I'm not convinced that our new millennium's "constant availability" is good news. I view it as yet another added distraction that nudges us away from living by our intuition and honoring our instinct. But then, I have always been amazed at friends who order a crisp chilled salad with iced tea on a winter's day, while I sit searching the menu for a bowl of robust hot soup and a buttery muffin.

I love the change of seasons and the distinctly varied pleasures that arrive with each transition. I feel more alive and connected when I pay attention to my body and its seasonal response to the earth's dance with the sun. I am not advocating a stringent regimen here. I actually resist restrictive diets and food rules. It fires up my inner goddess in protest! What I do think is important is to trust our own body's intuition, and pay attention to its natural response to changing weather, lunar phases, and seasonal influences.

For instance, let's think about a favorite soup. A classic potato soup, prepared steaming hot with the warming kiss of nutmeg, soothes us body and soul in the colder months of winter's sleep. In summer, the very same soup, minus the nutmeg, may be chilled and served with a topping of freshly snipped mint or chives. One soup is comforting and nurturing, the other is cooling and uplifting. But it's basically the same recipe. It's a simple yet powerful concept.

Cooking by moonlight is about making conscious food choices in harmony with the seasons and moon phases. It's about trusting our body to gravitate toward the kinds of nourishment it needs most. With that in mind, lets look at the four seasons and learn what Mother Nature has to teach us about appropriate nourishment.

Foods for Winter Moons

In the colder months of winter's gray robe, our bodies need the sustenance and comfort of grounding earthy foods and warming spices. Our energy is turned inward, toward survival and introspection, nurturing the inward journey of the soul. As the days shorten and give way to longer nights, we enter the Crone aspect of the Goddess. The earth is asleep in the grip of winter's freeze. Both body and spirit need protection and grounding—nourishment for the long dark passage of the north.

During the winter season, support your body with grounding foods and warming herbs and spices. Simmering soups and stews, chili, baked polentas and savory Southwestern dishes, herb-roasted chicken and root vegetables in rosemary oil, warm apple crisp, spicy squash pie, mugs of mulled cider, and hot chocolate stirred with a cinnamon stick all encourage nurture and support to body and soul.

Winter Herbs and Spices

Herbs and spices that are especially supportive during the winter moons are those that warm the body, ignite digestion, and boost immunity. Magically, these same foods, herbs, and spices help to protect and bring comfort, abundance, and healing. Many call upon the fire element. Following is a list of particular foods, herbs, and spices that you will find especially supportive during this darker time of year.

Allspice, anise, apples, bay, beans, broccoli, broth, Brussels sprouts, buttermilk, cabbage, canned tomatoes, caraway, carrots, casseroles, cauliflower, celery seed, chamomile tea, chili pepper, chocolate, cinnamon, cloves, coconut milk, coriander, corn, cornmeal, cranberries, cumin, currents, curry, dried basil, eggs, fennel, garlic, ground ginger, ginger root, hot beverages and teas, lemon, mace, maple syrup, molasses, nutmeg, oatmeal, olives, onions, oranges, oregano, parsley, pastas, pears, peppercorns, peppermint, pomegranates, Portobello mushrooms, potatoes, puddings, pumpkin, raisins, rice, risotto, roasted meals (fish, meats, vegetables), root vegetables, rosemary, sage, salmon, sea salt, sesame seeds, soups, spinach, star anise, stews, sweet marjoram, sweet potato, tarragon, thyme, tofu, turmeric, vanilla, winter savory, winter squashes, yogurt.

Foods for Spring Moons

As the earth's dance with the sun begins to lengthen our days, awaken green shoots, and urge our feathered sisters to weave their nests, we rediscover the Goddess in her Maiden aspect, drenched with life and newness, fresh and expectant. Our own bodies stretch and ache to move, to run wild, to inhale the green and vibrant energy of spring. Nourishment becomes stimulating and clarifying as we sweep out the cobwebs and accumulated stasis of winter.

Foods take on a different twist, changing from the comfort of earthy baked suppers to the astringent bite of watercress in salads, and lemon drizzled over baby spears of spring asparagus. Soups are vibrant, quick, and fresh, topped with citrusy chopped cilantro or sprigs of mint. Fish is poached in dry white wine and strewn with dill, and pastas are lavished with primavera vegetables and peppery basil leaves. Flavors awaken the senses and spark desire. The Green Man of the wildwood is returning to the forest. Maiden and maternal goddesses alike become flushed with desire. Energy becomes extroverted, urging us to connect, express, and grow.

Spring Herbs and Spices

Herbs and spices that are especially supportive during the spring moons are those that invigorate the body, awaken the senses, and cleanse the immune system. Magically, these same foods, herbs, and spices help to purify, stimulate, arouse, and heal. Many call upon the fire and air elements. Following is a list of particular foods, herbs, and spices that you will find especially supportive and magical during this heady time of rebirth.

Almond, apricot, anise, artichoke, asparagus, avocado, banana, basil, beans, bitter greens, cabbage, cantaloupe, capers, caraway, cardamom, carrots, chamomile, chervil, chili pepper, cilantro, coconut, coconut milk, coriander, cumin, curry, dandelion greens, dill, eggs, endive, fennel, fish, garlic, ginger root, grape, grapefruit, green beans, herb teas, honey, juices, Johnny-jump-ups, lavender, lemon, lemon balm, lemon thyme, lime, mesclun salad, mushrooms, mustard greens, new potatoes, olives, orange, oregano, pansies, parsley, pastas, peas, peppercorns, peppermint, pine nuts, rhubarb, rice, risotto, rosemary, salad greens, salmon, savory, sea salt, sesame seeds, sorbet, spearmint, spinach, spring onions, sweet marjoram, tarragon, thyme, tofu, turmeric, vanilla, violets, watercress, yogurt.

Foods for Summer Moons

By Midsummer we are in the thick of the Goddess' gifts. The days are long and warmed by her consort the Sun God, high in the sky. The Oak King is in his glory, the land is green and abounding with life. Herbs are ready for their first dawn harvest, gardens are exuberant with growing vegetables and faery roses. It is a time for weddings, graduations, and celebrations. The pursuit of love and pleasure is honored as a joyful part of life.

Foods are now at the peak of freshness, flavors are bold and sensuous. Appetizers are spicy, and soups are chilled with dollops of sour cream and freshly cut chives. Fish is grilled, and chicken is marinated in heavenly herbal oils and balsamic vinegar. Peppers of every color are fire roasted. Eating is moved outdoors as cotton tablecloths are tossed over weathered picnic tables. Wine is iced in coolers alongside brown bottles of barley brew and root beer.

Take pleasure now in the casual, the spontaneous, the simple: the gift of a ripe strawberry dipped in a saucer of brown sugar; the luxury of being barefoot; the early morning murmur of the doves. The Goddess is alive, and magic is astir. Seize each day and make food a celebration. How many summers will you experience? Now is the only moment we know.

Summer Herbs and Spices

Herbs and spices that are especially supportive during the summer moons are those that cool and refresh the body, invigorate the senses, and gently support the immune system. Magically, these same foods, herbs, and spices help to arouse passions and pleasure, and to celebrate and heal. Many call upon the air element, and some call upon the fire element. Following is a list of foods, herbs, and spices that you will find especially agreeable and magical during this time of warmth and abundance.

Almond, anise, apricot, artichoke, asparagus, avocado, banana, basil, beans, bell peppers, blackberries, blueberries, borage, cantaloupe, capers, caraway, cardamom, chamomile, cherries, chili pepper, chives, chocolate, cilantro, coconut, coconut milk, coriander, corn, cranberry, cucumber, cumin, curry, dill, eggplant, eggs, endive, fennel, fish, garlic, ginger root, grape, grilled fish, meat and vegetables, ice cream, iced tea, juices, lavender, lemon, lemon balm, lemon thyme, lemonade, lime, mangoes, marigolds, mesclun salad, mushrooms, nectarines, olives, oregano, parsley, pastas, pea pods, peaches, pecans, peppercorns, peppermint, pine nuts, pineapple, Portobello mushrooms, potatoes, raspberries, romaine, rice, risotto, rose petals, rosemary, sea salt, salad greens, sesame seeds, sorbet, spearmint, spinach, strawberries, summer savory, sun tea, sweet marjoram, tarragon, thyme, tofu, tomatoes, turmeric, vanilla, watercress, watermelon, yellow squash, yogurt, zucchini, zucchini flowers.

Foods for Autumn Moons

As the harvest is gathered and the earth's bounty celebrated, the moon rises golden and heavy. Birds mark the sky in their arrow-shaped instinct. Frost is around the corner, the dark time is coming. But not today. Today the Goddess breathes her burnished breath upon the land, spinning straw into gold. This is the Crone's alchemy, her last turn at beauty etched in wisdom, bittersweet. It is a time for noticing the small things, such as the creatures preparing for the colder nights ahead; it is a time of sleep and prophesy; it is a time for gathering—gathering strength, wisdom, patience, and sustenance.

Foods now become strengthening, boosting the immune system with earthy root vegetables and harvest flavors, restorative spices and herbs. Slow-cooked stews and lemon-roasted chicken nurture the spirit and support the body. Freshly baked breads, and muffins laced with cinnamon fill the house with the fragrance of the harvest. The Goddess' favored apples abound in an array of colors and textures, tempting us into the kitchen to conjure up batters for breads, cakes, and pies, comfort foods to face the shortening daylight.

The kitchen truly becomes the soul and center of the home during this wistful season, as Hestia, goddess of the hearth, moves quietly into our hearts. She teaches us patience and the art of centering, the art of being, and knowing. It is a time to go within and cultivate our intuition, a time to reflect upon our connection to our ancestors, a time to collect a new stack of books and put the tea kettle on. It's important to feed the imagination as well as the body.

Autumn Herbs and Spices

Herbs and spices that are especially supportive during the autumn moons are those that warm us and nurture the spirit, comfort the senses, and boost the immune system. Magically, these same foods, herbs, and spices bring sustenance and healing, protection and psychic support. Many call upon the water, fire, and air elements. Following is a list of particular foods, herbs, and spices that you will find especially comforting and magical during this time of dwindling light.

Acorn squash, almond, anise, apples, bay, beans, bell peppers, broccoli, Brussels sprouts, cabbage, canned tomatoes, capers, caraway, cardamom, carrots, casseroles, cauliflower, celery seed, chamomile, chili pepper, chocolate, cider, cilantro, cinnamon, cloves, coconut, coconut milk, coriander, corn, cornmeal, cranberry, cumin, currents, curry, dill, dried basil, eggplant, eggs, fennel, fish, garlic, ginger root, grape, hot herbal teas, lemon thyme, lime, mangoes, mace, maple, mesclun salad, molasses, mushrooms, nutmeg, nuts, olives, onions, orange, oregano, parsley, pastas, pears, pecans, peppercorns, pesto, pine nuts, Portobello mushrooms, potatoes, pumpkin, pumpkin seeds, raisins, rice, risotto, roasted fish, meat and vegetables, rosemary, sage, salad greens, sea salt, sesame seeds, spinach, soups, stuffing, sunflower seeds, sweet marjoram, sweet potatoes, tarragon, thyme, tofu, tomatoes, turmeric, vanilla, walnuts, wild rice, winter squash, yams, yogurt.

LOVE FOODS AND PRACTICAL MAGIC

Cooking is a sensual experience, and every wise woman inherently understands the seductive energy stirred within while creating a meal to share with a loved one. It's no accident that our grandmothers instructed us with the axiom "The way to a man's heart is through his stomach." Recent perfume surveys revealed that men actually preferred culinary scents over floral fragrances. Pumpkin pie and vanilla were chosen most often as the two sexiest scents!

Food, after all, is meant to be shared and savored. Tastes, textures, and delicious aromas delight and arouse the psyche. Sharing a meal becomes a natural form of communication, a way to invoke our bodily selves and surrender to the generosity of our five senses.

With this in mind, I've gathered together some appropriate food choices for the gentle art of seduction—foods believed to enhance feelings of love, sensuality, and pleasure.

Apples: Aphrodite's association with apples is legendary. With a natural affinity for the seductive flavors of cinnamon, nutmeg, and vanilla, this versatile fruit can be baked in pies, crisps, and cakes, sautéed with brandy, or brewed as warming spiced cider. Encourage your inner Aphrodite and rustle up an apple pie.

Apricots: Juicy golden apricots are considered fruits of love in goddess lore. Try serving apricots and almonds for a simple dessert to elevate amorous feelings. Belly dancing is optional.

Asparagus: I'm not sure how asparagus got its reputation as an aphrodisiac, but I do know that when prepared with loving care, just barely braised, still firm, bright green, and tender-crisp, they evoke thoughts of the Green Man and the return of spring.

Avocado: Associated with beauty, lust, and love, avocados are a sensual fruit. Spice up a guacamole with fiery chilies, lemon, and garlic for a seductive love appetizer.

Balsamic Vinegar: You may not find this staple listed elsewhere under love foods, unless you happen to be talking with an Italian goddess from Modena . . . she will understand! There is something powerfully seductive about a good, aged balsamic vinegar that transforms simple cheeses, roasted vegetables, and ripe fruits into a divinely sensual experience. Trust me.

Banana: Properties of bananas are said to invoke fertility, potency, and prosperity. Add cinnamon and vanilla in a home-baked banana bread, and you just might have a winner.

Barley: Folklore tells us that barley aids healing, love, and protection. It's also a perfect cleansing food for the waning moon. Stir up a barley soup in your favorite pot, and add appropriate spices to clear away old hurts and renew good will.

Beans: Make a reconciliation chili with a mixture of beans, onion, garlic, and bay leaf to protect your relationship and renew love. Add oregano for peace, happiness, and harmony.

Blueberry: Used for protection, blueberries can be powerful love food when baked with cinnamon in an old-fashioned crisp, or stirred into batter with vanilla for morning pancakes or a deliciously tempting blueberry bread.

Brazil Nuts: A fruit of the endangered rain forest, you can conjure feelings of love *and* help save our planet by serving Brazil nuts with your full moon celebrations.

Capers: A staple in my own pantry, capers are a distinctive salty accent to many Italian and Mediterranean dishes. They help bring luck, lust, and potency. Combine them with olive oil, lemon, garlic, and angel hair pasta for a seductive dinner under the stars.

Carrots: They're not only good for you, they're sexy. Steam them in orange juice, or toss them with fresh basil for a powerful love food.

Celery: The humble celery plant is thought to enhance mental powers as well as lust. Think about that the next time you toss together a tuna salad.

Cherries: Red or black, cherries bring a delightful sensation of sour and sweet. They invoke love and divination powers. Share a bowl of cherries with your lover and you may see visions of your future together.

Chervil: Used as an invigorating tonic, fresh chervil is a perfect addition to your spring salads. It also invites conscious awareness. And we all desire consciousness in love, don't we?

Chestnuts: Long associated with love, add chestnuts to your holiday stuffing to invite more affection into your family celebration. Add some chopped apples, cardamom, and thyme, and you'll invite friendship, healing, and happiness to your gathering.

Chili Peppers: Hot and spicy, reflecting the fire element, use the heat of chilies to enhance feelings of love and desire. Serve with frozen margaritas and watch your passions rise. Add chili pepper to hot chocolate and stir up some trouble. They are also associated with fidelity and hex breaking.

Chocolate: The cocoa bean is a true gift from the Dark Goddess. Share anything chocolate with a lover and you'll transcend the mundane to revel in the rich dark realm of sensuality. Indulge together often. Every good witch deserves chocolate.

Coconut: Perhaps because it has a tropical origin, I always associate coconut with pleasure and sensuality. Try cooking with coconut milk in soups and sauces. Add flaked coconut to fruit salads or chocolate desserts and hot curries. Pairing spicy and sweet flavors creates a highly sensual experience.

Corn: Not technically classified as a love food, corn usually emanates abundance, luck, and protection. But sharing a bowl of hot buttered popcorn with a lover is one of my favorite acts of seduction.

Endive: Who would have thought that this humble green that graces our salad plates could be a food of love and lust? Make a love salad of endive, grapes, apples, and mint with crumbles of chèvre.

Figs: Dark, sticky, and highly erotic, figs have conjured up thoughts of female sexuality for centuries. Share a plate of figs with your lover and see if this ancient fruit lives up to its reputation. Or indulge yourself with a bottle of fig balsamic vinegar, and heighten passions with a mere shake of your wrist.

Garlic: So many properties are associated with garlic. Luckily, lust is one of them. I can attest that eating copious amounts of garlic while in Italy for my honeymoon convinced me that garlic should forever be a staple in my kitchen.

Grapes: With connections to Dionysus, wine, and fertility, grapes are an erotic fruit of the Goddess and God. For full effect, serve with assorted cheeses, goblets of wine, and evocative music beneath the light of a waxing moon.

Lavender: Long regarded as an evocation of higher spiritual love, many wise women grow lavender and toss the tiny buds into recipes for that extra special secret ingredient. Try mixing a pinch or two of lavender buds into softened lemon sorbet for a refreshing Midsummer love treat.

Lemons and Limes: There is something absolutely delightful about the fresh taste and tart fragrance of citrus. Both lemons and limes evoke love, and I recommend using them liberally, squeezing their juice on everything from cooked pastas to fresh salads, sliced fruits, broiled fish, and drinks both hot and iced. And don't forget their magic in baked goodies.

Mangoes: A highly sensual and erotic fruit long associated with love and passion, share a ripe mango in bed with your lover on a sultry afternoon. If you happen to be alone, share a mango with yourself. You'll be glad you did.

Marigold: Sprinkle marigold petals (unsprayed and pesticide-free) in any food you wish to enhance with intentions of ardor. Pair marigold with garlic for adding flames of passion.

Olives: Associated more with the Goddess Athena than Aphrodite, I still find sharing olives and a glass of wine with a lover a sensual experience. Magically, olives bring us security, marriage, and fidelity in love. Ah, that may be why my lover is also my husband . . .

Oranges: Bright and fresh, lively and refreshing, oranges are evocative of love, abundance, and happiness. Use them liberally. They are liquid sunshine.

Papaya: Soothing to the tummy, a natural aid in digestion, papaya is also associated with love. Serve your lover fresh or dried papaya after a particularly indulgent meal, and you may just thank the Goddess later.

Passion Fruit: Need I say more?

Peaches: The quintessential taste of summer, ripened peaches are so evocative of sensuality and the Goddess it's no wonder we think of them as a fruit of love. Paired with fresh cream and brown sugar, peaches invoke beauty and lust.

Pears: Although somewhat more austere than a dripping peach, pears are also love fruits and their natural sugary sweetness will bring a slow smile to your lover's lips. Serve with snowy chèvre for a simple, sensuous appetizer. Feed each other.

Pineapple: A sweet and sensual fruit invoking visions of paradise, pineapple brings luck and prosperity. Bake a love cake with pineapple, vanilla, and ginger, and serve it to your loved ones. Perfect for any holiday.

Plums: A sensuous summer love fruit, juicy and sweet. Bring a blanket, your lover, and plenty of plums with you and have an afternoon picnic. Choose a secluded spot.

Raspberries: Love-inducing raspberries have a fragile elegance that they impart to desserts. As whole berries, or crushed in sauces, or paired with chocolate, lemon cake, or coconut cream, raspberries are a serious love food!

Rice: Long associated with fertility, rice can also be love food when cooked with seductive spices, vegetables, and fruits. Toss rice with mint, lemon, and sautéed carrots for such an effect. When you need comfort for lost love, stir yourself up a warm rice pudding with vanilla and cinnamon.

Roses: Long associated with the essence of love, strew unsprayed and organic rose petals in fruit salads, punch, and platters of desserts. Stir chopped petals into softened ice creams or float them on a pool of cream beneath a dark, rich brownie. Your lover will swoon.

Sesame Seeds: Besides adding a satisfying crunch to stir-fried veggies or roasted potatoes, sesame seeds invoke lust and money. A rather nice magical combination, don't you think?

Strawberries: Recipe for a sensuous Sunday: luscious ripe, juicy strawberries rolled in soft brown sugar and dipped in sour cream, served in bed, on a plate between you and your lover, sky-clad. Sunday paper is optional.

Sweet Potatoes: Who knew? Whip up some baked sweet potatoes with a little coconut milk, add a dash of cinnamon and ginger, and you'll be bringing love food to your dinner table.

Tomatoes: Long associated with the goddesses Venus and Aphrodite, red juicy tomatoes are indeed a perfect love food. Paired with other sensual and lusty flavors such as garlic, basil, mint, and olive oil, tomatoes can create a desire for passion and a deeper appreciation for the sensual side of life.

NOTES FROM A MOONLIT KITCHEN

Food Choices Make a Difference

We've come a long way from the 1960s fashion of smothering everything in condensed cream soups. As health- and taste-conscious cooks demand fresher, more diverse foods, the entire food marketplace is impacted, influencing everything from the way we shop to the way we prepare our meals. Family cooks everywhere are experimenting with new flavors, expanding their palates with a new appreciation for world cuisine, fresh herbs, and exotic spices. Once difficult to find items such as coconut milk, Thai rice noodles, chèvre, aged balsamic vinegar, or polenta can now be found in most supermarkets. New businesses committed to offering natural foods, organic dairy and produce, free-range chickens, and hormone-free eggs are cropping up everywhere.

For all cooks and goddesses seeking to live in harmony with Mother Earth, honoring her seasonal offerings, this is good news indeed. Politics aside, *it's simply better* for our bodies, our planet, and our collective future. Wise women recognize that Mother Earth sustains us. Wise women recycle. Wise women care about where our food comes from.

Food as Energy

If we identify ourselves as lovers of the earth and the Goddess, we must naturally look at our food choices. As we become more aware of how energy works, we begin to understand that an aerosol can of artificial Cheez Whiz is not going to contain *life* energy! We are what we eat. Food is more than just fuel, it is essence . . . and our own body's energy system is affected by our food choices on deep levels. Think about the integrity of your body the next time you're habitually reaching for a diet soda. What elemental energy are you inviting into your body? Begin making more conscious food choices. Wise women eat consciously.

Going Organic

As a woman and mother on the Goddess path, I feel it is imperative that we support our organic farmers, who bravely challenge corporate trends, often risking financial certainty for the sake of their conviction in untainted food sources. By purchasing organic and natural products whenever possible, supporting those who break new and unpolluted ground, we will slowly but surely impact how our foods are grown. This is a consumer-based culture, after all, and each one of us has buying *power*. We can, through our daily habitual choices, influence trends and create more demand for truly wholesome foods.

I overheard a loud protest in the supermarket the other day: a woman was complaining about "affording the higher cost" of organic produce. I turned to look, glancing into the face of a small child sitting in the vocal mother's cart. Gazing into those young eyes, the answer, for me, is simple. How can we afford *not* to?

Surely our food budget can be rearranged to support more wholesome organic foods. There's always room for a better choice. Start with milk and eggs, then poultry and meats. They contain high amounts of antibiotics, growth hormones, and pesticides, and are an excellent first choice for going organic.

Whenever possible, stock up on organic sale items. Markets will periodically feature specials on organic labels. I can often find organic beans, juices, soups, and canned tomatoes on sale in a regular supermarket. And when I do, I stock up. Choose organic fresh vegetables and fruits whenever you can afford to. Look for labels sporting "No GMO's" (genetically modified ingredients). I find that the impact on my food budget is less and less an issue as I become more focused on making wholesome choices rather than choices based on impulse and convenience.

Body Image and Eating Intuitively

When I speak of wholesome foods, I am not defining foods in moral terms, or including the concept of "diet." Rather, I am attempting to pare down to a very simple concept . . .

We are what we eat . . . and food is energy.

In our consumer-focused culture, we are deluged with words like *"diet"* and *"calories," "fat grams"* and *"carbohydrates."* We are constantly persuaded through advertising that a carefully regimented diet of *"light"* foods and *"low-fat"* meals is the equivalent of health. We are encouraged to obsess about the number of calories and cringe at fat grams. We are emotionally supported to assign negative attributes to foods we desire. How many of us routinely label one food *"bad"* and another food *"good"*? Now, think for a moment about how absurd that truly is. Chocolate cake is "devil's food" while oat bran muffins are a "healthy choice"?

This way of thinking finds many of us caught up in a cycle of self-denial, eventually giving in to so-called *temptation,* only to feel *guilty* for our lack of self-discipline. All that energy and focus invested in a simple slice of chocolate cake! Most certainly not a healthy approach, and definitely not a *pleasurable* one. We all need to resist the negative messages about food in our culture.

Let us relax, breathe deeply, and reject the barrage of images touting so-called perfection. Let us cultivate more balance in our everyday choices. Let us regain control of our own body image . . . and toss out the fashion catalogues! Most of all, let us regain a sense of our own bodies' intuition. The starving models in underwear ads have denied every ounce of their body's instinct. They have trained their hunger, chemically restrained their appetite, and lost their vitality. Why do we worship them? The truth is, most women don't. Most men don't. The media does. Turn the media off.

The Denial of Pleasure

At a recent gathering I was laughing with a friend about my predictable cyclic desire for chocolate as we stood chatting and eating chocolate chip brownies. A woman nearby scolded us. She told us that we "craved the chocolate during PMS because our bodies needed the mineral manganese," and neatly informed us that she simply takes her manganese in a pill every morning, triumphantly declaring, "I never eat chocolate." My friend and I looked at each other with a silent, mutual glimmer, knowing just what the other was thinking: *Oh, please! Let us just enjoy the chocolate.*

Why have chocolate and certain other foods become forbidden? After all, foods and fruits of the earth are not either inherently *"bad"* or innately *"good."* Even apples can be problematic. An apple a day supposedly keeps the doctor away . . . but an uncooked apple gives me a painful stomachache. I cannot digest them. Does that mean that apples are *bad*? Certainly not. It simply means that *my* body needs the apples cooked, while *yours* may vibrate with joy at the crunch of a raw Granny Smith. The answer lies within; pay attention to your own body, and its inherent intuition.

The electronic barrage of advertising and its promotion of our pop-cultural obsession with the icon of perfection have influenced all of us, affecting our values, our body image, and our personal associations to food. Diet-conscious women may buy "fat-free" fudge-covered cookies in an attempt to reduce fat calories, only to find themselves eating the entire box in one evening because the cookies never truly satisfy their hunger. Their artificiality leaves them starved for *real* food.

A friend of mine from Israel who owns a new bakery in Massachusetts commented to me that he has never before witnessed such guilt-ridden discussions about food. "Women always talk about the calories," he said. "Twenty minutes later, they're still talking. They give in, buy the slice of cake, then they're back here the next day, having the same conversation." My friend just shakes his head.

We have strayed far from the Garden of Eden. Our natural connection to the earth has been eroded. We have lost touch with the ebb and flow of our instincts. Our intuition has been culturally persuaded to go underground.

Another woman I know wrestled daily with her self-imposed diet. She ran seven miles a day and ate a regimen so fat free that she began to feel ill. Upon examination, her doctor concluded that she wasn't ingesting *enough* fat. He prescribed for her the following prescription: two tablespoonfuls of extra virgin olive oil a day. She dutifully complied, swallowing her two tablespoonfuls every morning, like daily medicine. Rather than taking pleasure in the olive oil drizzled on a toasted slice of garlicky bread or swirled into a bowl of freshly made soup, my friend chose to *take her medicine,* still viewing the olive oil as fat, her sworn enemy—its sensual pleasure denied rather than simply and naturally enjoyed.

The Lie of Perfection

We all have our personal food issues to wrestle with. Food is closely tied to our concept of mother, nurturance, and comfort. It is rare indeed that someone completely escapes some circumstantial influence around the issue of food. Whether our eating style is denial or overindulgence, you can count on familial issues at work. As a daughter, woman, and mother, I struggle daily to differentiate my authentic self from external expectations. I fight to hear my intuition amidst the clamor and pressure of society's collective influence. Like many adult women, I have had to relearn the relationship between food and pleasure.

When I was child, food was fraught with family issues. Carving out my own path and discovering kinship with the Goddess has nurtured my childhood wounds. I have discovered deeper wisdom by letting go of our culture's lie of perfection. Writing my first goddess cookbook was a profound, remarkable process of healing, a move toward personal authenticity and empowerment.

I continue on that journey toward authenticity, exploring the sensual in foods and celebrating the diversity of seasonal nourishment. I turn to the Goddess' moon to guide me back to the garden: back to intuition, back to our spiral cyclic nature, and back to the significant honesty and value of allowing ourselves pleasure, and honoring both body and spirit.

It is my heartfelt belief that if we let go of society's collective control of our body image and our relationship to food, we will return to a more natural, instinctive approach to cooking and nourishment. We will be better fed, both physically and spiritually. Our own body's wisdom will lead us to balance.

If we truly pay attention to our intuition, our body's signals, and our personal appetites, without judgment and without imposing our culture's masks of virtue and desirability, we open ourselves and find our *own* ideal, free to become our distinctive reflection of the Goddess in all her varied shapes, sizes, and colors.

My hope in offering you this collection of seasonal recipes and lunar musings is that you open your heart to love yourself and are inspired to cook with pleasure and magic, exulting in the bounty of the Great Goddess herself. Her wisdom is held softly within your very center, your body's intuition, your quiet inner voice. Gaze at the moon and listen deeply. Join me in reclaiming feminine intuition and cooking by moonlight.

STOCKING A MOONLIT PANTRY

Keeping an abundance of key ingredients handy makes life in the kitchen a more creative and spontaneous experience. If you have choices at your fingertips, your creativity will flow.

A Note Regarding Ingredients

The thing is, I would love to tell you that I make my own broth from scratch, that I plan well enough in advance to soak my dried beans overnight, and that I can my own tomatoes. But the truth is, I enjoy convenience in the kitchen as much as any modern woman.

When it comes to cooking, I love fresh, wholesome ingredients, freshly picked herbs, organic free-range eggs, and the best balsamic vinegar I can get my hands on outside of Modena. But I am also (like most women I know) a practical cook. My day is filled with work projects: writing, painting, and research, not to mention mothering and being a passionate wife to my devoted husband . . . so something has to give. And it's not going to be the writing or the other things . . . trust me. It's going to be the bean soaking thing.

To be honest, I wonder if most of us living outside of the metropolitan San Francisco or New York area could actually tell the difference between a bean soaked overnight and a good organic brand from a can. Perhaps a true foodie has a nose for such things. But when push comes to shove, I'm more prone to invoke Aphrodite than a celebrity chef.

I'm interested in an array of edible pleasures, yes. But I'm also interested in having the time to take a long walk in the woods and paint the early evening sky. Although great eating is high on my list, so is the pursuit of love and beauty. And I haven't heard any complaints that I'm not soaking my beans.

My advice is simply to choose the freshest seasonal ingredients you can find, and buy organic whenever possible. If you keep your kitchen well stocked with the staples listed below and on the following pages, you'll have culinary magic right at your fingertips. Creating meals intuitively is much easier when the ingredients are handy.

Choose organic products whenever possible. (See appendix A for ordering information.)

Apples (in season)

Apple cider vinegar

Apple juice or cider (in season)

Artichokes (canned, jarred, or frozen)

Avocados

Baked beans (canned)

Baking powder

Baking soda

Balsamic vinegar (aged at least five to seven years)

Bananas

Barbecue sauce (the best you can buy)

Black olives (ripe, canned)

Black-eyed peas (canned or frozen)

Bread crumbs (seasoned)

Broth (chicken and vegetable)

Butter (salted or unsalted)

Canned beans (organic, if possible):

    black beans

    chili beans

    chickpeas (garbanzo)

    great northern beans (white beans)

    kidney beans (dark and light)

    pinto beans

Canned green chilies (whole and chopped)

Capers

Catsup

Cheeses:

    asiago

    blue cheese (or Saga)

    cheddar

    chèvre

    cream cheese (or Neufchâtel)

    Emmenthaler

    feta

    Gruyère

    Monterey Jack

    mozzarella

    Parmesan (or Parmigiano-Reggiano)

    ricotta

    Romano (or pecorino)

    Swiss

Chicken broth (organic, free-range)

Chili oil

Chili sauce

Chips (yellow and blue corn)

Chocolate chips (semisweet and flavored)

Cocoa (unsweetened)

Coconut milk (canned, unsweetened)

Coffee beans (gourmet or organic)

Condensed milk (sweetened)

Corn (frozen)

Cornmeal (stone-ground)

Cornstarch

Couscous

Cranberries (sweetened, dried)

Cranberry juice

Currants (dried)

Curry paste (green and red)

Dijon mustard

Eggs (free-range, organic, and local)

Flour (unbleached organic, all-purpose)

Fruit (assorted, in season)

Fruit (jarred)

Garlic (fresh . . . lots of it!)

Ginger root (fresh)

Gluten-free flours (for those who cannot eat wheat)

Granola

Green chilies

Green olives (Spanish)

Greek olives (kalamata)

Grits (quick-cooking)

Half-and-half (half milk and half cream, or nondairy cream)

Herbs and spices:

   basil leaves (fresh and dried)

   bay leaf

   caraway seeds

   cayenne pepper (ground)

   celery seed

   chamomile

   chili powder

   chives (fresh)

   cilantro (fresh)

   cinnamon (stick and ground)

   cloves (whole buds and ground)

   coriander seeds

   cumin (ground and whole seeds)

   curry powder (mild and hot)

   dill (fresh and dried)

   fennel seeds

   fenugreek

   ginger (ground and fresh root)

   Italian herbs (dried)

   lavender buds

lemon balm (fresh)

lemon pepper

lemon thyme (fresh)

marjoram (sweet marjoram)

mint (fresh)

nutmeg (whole)

oregano (fresh or dried)

parsley (curly or flat-leafed, and fresh)

peppercorns (black, white, red, green)

red pepper flakes

rosemary (fresh is best)

sage (dried, rubbed)

tarragon (dried)

thyme (fresh is best)

Honey (local and organic)

Horseradish (prepared)

Juice concentrates (frozen, orange, lime)

Lemonade

Lemons

Limes

Maple syrup (pure)

Mayonnaise

Milks (organic dairy, almond, rice, soy)

Molasses

Mustards (honey and spicey)

Nuts:

almonds

hazelnuts

peanuts

pecans

pine nuts

pistachios

walnuts

Oats (quick-cooking and regular)

Olive oil (extra virgin and light)

Onions (assorted: red, yellow, sweet, spring, Vidalia)

Oranges

Orange juice

Pasta (made in Italy, Italian semolina, or gluten-free):

angel hair

farfalle

fettuccini

lasagna noodles

linguini

penne

ravioli (keep frozen)

rigatoni

spaghetti

tortellini (cheeses, chicken, et cetera; keep frozen)

ziti

Pasta sauce (jarred)

Pears (in season)

Peanut butter (natural)

Peanut oil (keep refrigerated)

Peas (frozen)

Piecrusts (both dough and graham cracker crusts)

Pizza shell or Italian flatbread (such as Boboli)

Polenta (stone-ground, regular or instant)

Potatoes (Idaho, New, Red, Sweet, Yukon Gold, et cetera)

Preserves (assorted fruit)

Pumpkin (canned)

Raisins (golden and regular)

Rice:

    arborio

    basmati or jasmine

    brown (short- and long-grained)

    pilaf mix

    Texmati (Texas-grown version of basmati)

    wild rice

Roasted red peppers (jarred)

Salad dressings

Salad greens (mesclun, romaine, et cetera)

Salmon (canned)

Salsa (jarred, mild, medium, and hot, green and red)

Sea salt

Sesame oil

Sherry (dry, and the real thing, not "cooking sherry")

Sherry vinegar

Shrimp (frozen, large)

Soy sauce (or wheat-free tamari)

Sour cream

Sparkling water

Stir-fry sauces (mild and hot)

Sugar (brown, confectioners', granulated)

Sun-dried tomatoes

Tea:

    regular tea

    herb tea

Tofu (silken, firm, and soft)

Tomato sauce (canned, plain, or flavored)

Tomatoes (canned organic, crushed, cut, and whole)

Tomatoes (fresh, cherry, Roma, vine ripe, et cetera)

Tortillas (corn and flour)

Tuna (white albacore packed in olive oil or spring water)

Vanilla extract

Vegetable broth (organic)

Vegetable oils (canola, sunflower, safflower)

Vegetables (assorted, in season; organic when possible)

Vinegars (cider, cranberry, raspberry, rice, wine, et cetera)

Wine (red and white, for cooking)

Worcestershire sauce

Wraps (or tortilla-style flatbreads for sandwiches or pizzas)

Xanthan gum (thickener for ice creams and gluten-free baking)

Yeast (active)

Yogurt (plain, organic)

USING HERBS AND SPICES MAGICALLY

To begin cooking with intention, the first (and perhaps most important) truth is to understand the power of your own spirit and focus. You might gather reams of information and tools, read charts on corresponding attributes of various herbs and elements, purchase "properly colored" candles, and gather your herbs on the "correct" day . . . however, if your heart and soul is not invested in your intention, and you allow your ego to dictate your needs, your magic will not be as potent as it could be. The simplest heartfelt desire can be far more effective than the most elaborately crafted ritual. Homemade soup that is stirred with love, and breads that are baked with your heart's highest intention often contain much more of the wisdom and energy of the Goddess than any theatrical cookbook ceremony.

Thoughts on Love Spells

I have found that if you pare down your desire to its simplest form, you open your life to more possibility. Rather than creating a wish that becomes more and more specific and, therefore, more and more limiting, consider the whole realm of possibility, and leave plenty of room for the Goddess to work her magic.

For example, you may have a mad crush on some eye-catching coworker down the hall, and be tempted to create a brownie that will enslave his or her heart to yours. This may not be wise. You may not be privy to the fact that this comely soul still lives at home with a doting, controlling mother and is virtually incapable of experiencing joy or intimacy, while off in the distance, just out of sight, is a love worth waiting for. Rather than investing time and effort into specifics, focus on developing a self worthy of love, and open your heart to opportunity.

Invite love itself into your life. And that includes self-love. Have fun! Play music and dance as you stir. Murmur words that would make Aphrodite blush. Sing your heart's intention as you knead fresh bread dough, or fill your kitchen with laughter as you sprinkle herbs and spices.

Examine your heart and keep your purpose honorable. Respect others, and listen to your own intuition as you contemplate your desires. In the end, ritual cooking is about offering up a reverential prayer, seasoning foods with love and healing, and serving up your highest intentions for the greater good of all, using the humblest of tools and ingredients. Simple magic happens with the clearest intentions.

What Wise Women Know

In the past, Wise Women and gifted cooks were challenged to create delicious, healing, and nurturing foods from whatever they had on hand, often working with strict seasonal limitations and modestly appointed pantries. Our ready abundance today and appetite for instant meals have dulled our seasonal intuition and inhibited us from our natural connection to the Mother's cycles. It is time now to reconnect with our more straightforward origins of the archetypal Wise Woman and tune in to the inherent magic of simplicity, clarity, and intention.

As we begin to work with our food in a conscious manner, infusing our recipes with intention, remember that your ingredients need not be exotic, mysterious, or hard to find.

The most powerful tool in your ritual cupboard is your own heart.

Everyday herbs and spices paired with common ingredients can positively work magic in the kitchen when infused with your focus and strength of character. It is your highest, deepest self that contains your power. If you gently open to the energy of the Goddess, her attributes will come alive through you . . . you will become the essence of the feminine divine, and your recipes will vibrate with the love and magic you bring to them.

Herbs, Spices, Magical Foods

Always buy your spices fresh, in small quantities, and keep them in airtight containers away from sunlight, moisture, and heat.

Magical Moonlight Tips

Herbs and spices don't actually spoil, they lose their vibrancy, color, and strength. Expect to use your herbs and spices well within a year. Once their color and aroma have faded, it's time to replace the old with the new. Discard them during the waning moon with proper intention.

Remarkably, herbs and spices do not fair well in the freezer. Repeated removal for use in recipes only introduces humidity and air into the container, affecting the quality of flavor and scent.

Ground spices lose their flavor faster than whole spices. Storing spices whole increases their shelf life. Toast whole spices briefly in a hot, dry pan before crushing to bring out their depth of flavor. A traditional mortar and pestle will do the trick, and so will a clean coffee grinder.

A wise woman adds spices in the first phase of cooking a dish. Adding spices to your cooking oil as it warms will infuse the entire dish with flavor and magic. Stir clockwise and visualize your intention for a minute before proceeding.

A general rule about using herbs in cooking is to add *dried* herbs at the beginning and *fresh* herbs near the end. Fresh herbs are delicate. It is better to add fresh herbs near the completion of a dish for a burst of bright flavor.

Here is a suggested list of easy-to-find herbs, spices, and flavorings for cooking by moonlight:

Almond: Known and loved for its subtle seductive aroma, almond is associated with clearing the conscious mind, yet I have always linked its distinctive flavor to something more sensual. . . . Perhaps then it is an appropriate addition for an intention involving consciousness in matters of the heart.

Anise: A licorice-tasting herb associated with the air element, anise calms digestion and brings a touch of psychic awareness to foods, enhancing divination. It is also thought to be protective and purifying. Use fresh leaves in an herbal salad, or strewn on poached fish.

Basil: A beloved herb that infuses tomato-based dishes with lively, peppery aromatics, basil is uplifting, inducing feelings of love, passion, mental clarity, and harmony. Associated with the fire element, it is a must for any moonlit pantry. Keep both fresh and dried on hand. I use basil almost daily. It's perfect for pasta sauces, pesto, pizza, and tomato salads.

Bay Leaf: The leaf of the laurel has long been cherished as a symbol for consecration, protection, and healing. Associated with the fire element, use it whole in soups and sauces to infuse prosperity, love, and protection. In our house I leave the bay leaf in the pasta sauce as I serve it, and whoever encounters it in their dish is especially blessed; it's a spiritual door-prize, if you will. (Note: don't ingest the leaf, as it will cause indigestion and distress!)

Caraway Seed: The lovely distinctive flavor of caraway adds dimension to soda breads, potato salads, and many moon vegetables, such as cauliflower, cabbage, and potatoes. Associated with air, it imparts the magical qualities of fidelity and protection while also enhancing memory.

Cardamom: Linked to Venus, this sweet and delectable spice is a lovely addition to breads, cakes, and biscuits baked for intentions of love, sensuality, and passion. Make sure you buy only very fresh cardamom in a good spice store, as its delicate flavor quickly fades.

Celery Seed: Associated with the earth element, use celery seed in potato and tuna salads to help cleanse energy and cultivate psychic development.

Chamomile: A favorite flower used in teas to calm tummies and nerves, its bitter apple fragrance enhances relaxation and invites peace. It is associated with Venus and the element of water. Pair it with lavender and honey for a soothing tea.

Chervil: A tonic for the body, perfect as a springtime pick-me-up, use chervil in salads to invoke a clearing of the conscious mind.

Chili Pepper: Whether ground into powder or chopped into flakes, chili adds the fire element to everything from vegetables, pizza dough, cornbreads, Southwestern dishes, garlicky pastas, eggs, and beans. Chilies are believed to be curative, preventative, and passion inducing. So start a fire!

Cilantro: Next to parsley, cilantro is probably the most popular culinary herb. Associated with the fire element, its refreshing leaves are the perfect addition to spicy foods, salsas, and salads, attracting health, gain, fertility, and passion.

Cinnamon: One of the most popular spices, cinnamon can be used both in its stick (bark) form and ground form. Associated with both air and fire, use cinnamon to enhance feelings of love and abundance, and to attract success and induce passion. It equally complements both sweet and spicy dishes. Pair it with fruits for love, and winter squashes for warming. Infuse your cornbreads and muffins with the sweet smell of success.

Cloves: The tiny dried buds of a flower originally grown in China, whole cloves are often used to spice up teas and ciders. Add ground cloves to curries, pies, and quick breads. Associated with the fire element, cloves clear away negative energies and are useful for protection and peace of mind. I often keep a simmering pot of cloves on the stove during winter months to help dispel any stagnant energies trapped in the house.

Coriander: The orange-scented seeds of the herb plant known as cilantro, coriander adds the fire element to your dishes crafted for health, passion, protection, gain, and fertility. Use with vegetables, curries, and add to pickles.

Cumin: The scent of cumin is very sexy. Used often in Indian dishes and Southwestern recipes, cumin brings the element of fire and protection to chili, soups, salsas, chicken dishes, cole slaw, potato salads, and egg dishes. It's often my "secret ingredient" in seasonal soups, dips, and sauces.

Dill: The distinctive scent of dill is associated with both air and fire, and is most often used for love and protection. Added to your potato salad, cream cheese omelets, or baked fish, it's a wonderful way to bring blessings, protection, and confidence to your table.

Fennel: A perfect herb for any Midsummer feast, fennel infuses its properties of air and fire into your ritual cooking. Substitute freshly sliced fennel for celery in your familiar salad recipes. Use it to conjure courage, confidence, longevity, love, and gain.

Garlic: The infamous "stinking rose" has a lore and history that goes back centuries. A favorite in many a witch's kitchen, garlic brings the fire element to any dish, and imparts strong protective, passionate, and magical qualities. Use it liberally in cooking, rub cut cloves on your doorways and thresholds to stave off intruding negativity, and hang braids of garlic in stagnant corners.

Ginger: Fiery ginger root is a must-have in any moonlit kitchen. Ginger stimulates digestion, eases nausea and headaches, and invigorates the body as an all-around tonic. Use it in stir-fries, Asian noodle dishes, winter soups, fruit desserts, and fresh salsas to attract love, fire up passions, and psychically protect loved ones. Slice fresh ginger for a curative tea that helps colds, tummy upsets, and headaches.

Lavender: The clean and refreshing scent of lavender raises vibrational energies to a higher level. One of the most beloved all-around beneficial herbs, lavender is associated with air. It cures headaches, eases tension, and helps sleep and dreams. Baked in cookies, stirred into sorbets, and brewed as tea, lavender can invite true spiritual love and healing. Traditionally collected at Midsummer, it is a must-have in your garden, flower pot, or cupboard.

Lemon Balm: A delightful lemony herb associated with the element of air. Use leaves in poultry and fish dishes, fruit desserts, teas, and salads to invite peace and happiness. Its scent is said to help alleviate depression and uplift the spirit; pair it with lavender for a sweet-scented pillow-sachet.

Mace: A traditional holiday spice, mace is linked to the air element and is lovely in pies and baked goodies. Magically, it brings gain, good luck, love, and protection into the home.

Nutmeg: Both fire and air, nutmeg is a warming, heady spice that attracts money and love. Use it also for protection and clairvoyance in your autumn soups, pies, apple dishes, pumpkin recipes, and ice cream. Buy whole nutmegs and grate them fresh, as the potency and taste is incomparable.

Oregano: A cousin to the mint family, oregano imparts a distinctive flavor and fresh scent that enhances egg, tomato, and vegetable dishes with its air element. Add to soups, stews, pizza, and pasta to bring happiness, peace, and harmony. It also offers protection and supports one through grief.

Parsley: The natural breath freshener, parsley is sacred to Persephone. A powerful herb for cleansing, it is used for purification, psychic development, and divination. Its earth element makes it a perfect herb to invite luck and fertility. Use it in rice dishes, pastas, vegetables, omelets, and herb butters. Especially lovely when paired with lemon and garlic.

Peppercorns: Associated with the fire element, pepper is a stimulant, invigorating and irritating. Use it to spice up any dish infused with passion, or to protect oneself from the effects of envy. Considered to have spell-breaking properties as well.

Peppermint: Vibrating to Venus, peppermint is such a beneficial herb that I grow all the varieties I can get my hands on, from orange to pineapple, and even chocolate! Associated with the air element, mint is cleansing, healing, and reviving. It calms digestion and soothes nerves. Use it in stews, couscous, and grain and rice dishes. Pair it with grilled fish and toss it with pastas laced with lemon and garlic to invoke protection, and invite dreams, love, happiness, and prosperity. And don't forget the simple joy of peppermint tea, hot or iced.

Poppy Seed: Associated with the water element and vibrating to the moon, poppy seeds are purported to invite dreams and clairvoyance. Add them to muffins, breads, and cakes.

Rosemary: One of my favorite herbs, rosemary emanates the fire element and is linked to the sun. Its fresh, cleansing fragrance clears the mind and invigorates the body. Its associations are multiple and positive; use it to protect, heal, enhance memory, and invite passion, good luck, confidence, and healing. Infuse it in oils, bake it in breads, and sprinkle it on poultry and roasted vegetables. Keeping rosemary planted by the door helps protect your home. Burning sprigs cleanses the house of negativity and "clears the air."

Sage: Culinary-rubbed sage is linked to the earth element and enhances poultry, meat, stuffings, and roasted harvest vegetables with its dusky fragrance. Use it for cleansing, healing, longevity, wisdom, and domestic harmony. (Note: Desert sage [artemisia] is burned by Native Americans [called smudging] for its smoke, which is purifying, cleansing, and healing. It's a treasured favorite in my house, but is not to be ingested.)

Salt: I prefer using natural sea salt in my cooking and magical work. I love the texture and the sweeter flavor. Associated with the earth element, for some it also invokes water, due to its oceanic source. Use it in all foods to enhance flavors and invite protection. Use sea salt in the bath to help purify yourself.

Savory: Associated with air and the planet Venus, savory is a perfect addition to love foods, as it attracts love, happiness, sensuality, and virility. Use it fresh in poultry, bean, and vegetable dishes. Use summer savory during the warmer moons, and winter savory during the colder months.

Spearmint: Like peppermint, spearmint is refreshing, cleansing, and uplifting. An herb of Venus, linked to air, use it in intentions concerning love, happiness, prosperity, and passion. I enjoy mint teas every day, either hot or iced. Invite love and happiness daily!

Star Anise: An Asian spice with a distinctive licorice-like flavor, star anise invites dreams and clairvoyance. Associated with both air and water, use it to make a tea infusion for enhancing your dreams.

Sweet Marjoram: A beloved herb in Italian cooking, marjoram enhances love dishes featuring Venus' favorite: tomatoes. It is also tasty with vegetables and eggs. Its flavor is delicate, so add marjoram to your cooking at the last moment. Associated with the air element, use it to strengthen love, ease tension, and invite relaxation and happiness.

Tarragon: Associated with the fire element, tarragon is a lovely herb used often in French cooking. It invokes passion, confidence, strength, and protection. Add it to poultry, crab, egg dishes, and cream sauces. Also wonderful when infused in vinegar or olive oil.

Thyme: Linked to Venus and air, thyme is a sturdy grower in the garden, and I enjoy planting it in several varieties. Use thyme on steamed and roasted vegetables (lemon thyme is wonderful), as well as egg and poultry dishes to invite divination, dreams, cleansing, love, money, and happiness.

Turmeric: The striking color of curry powder comes from the intense golden pigment of turmeric. Associated with fire, it invokes courage, strength, sensuality, and magic. It is considered a tonic for the body. Use it in curries and stir-fries to invigorate and strengthen. It's also useful in breaking spells.

Vanilla: A most favored flavor and scent, the vanilla bean is actually an orchid seed pod, grown in warm and sensual climates. Associated with the fire element, it is a most useful spice in invoking passion and sensuality. In studies, vanilla was identified by men as one of the sexiest scents, after pumpkin pie. Yes, pumpkin pie! Now do you believe in cooking magic?

Other Edibles from the Garden

Certain flowers are edible as well as beautiful, and can add a touch of whimsy, or a magical vibrant accent to your salads, desserts, pastas, soups, and beverages. When you choose a blossom for your garnish, make sure that you know exactly where it came from. It must be pesticide-free, unsprayed, and organic. Very gently and briefly rinse the flower off and dry it lightly before you add it to your dish. Garnish just before serving.

Here is a goddess handful of edible flowers to accent your kitchen magic:

Lavender: The clean and heady fragrance of lavender is quite strong, so use it sparingly until you find just the right amount of flavoring for your taste buds. Lavender brings love and luck and a higher spiritual vibration to any intention. Add it to baked goods, or stir it into softened sorbets, ice creams, and frostings. Create lavender sugar by processing a few buds with granulated sugar in your food processor. Make an infusion for a lovely Midsummer tea and add a dab of honey, or create an herbal cream cheese by adding some freshly chopped lavender, rosemary, and mint.

Marigolds: The bitter and musky taste of marigold petals are associated with the fire element, and are perfect for any intention focusing on courage, protection, sexuality, and health. French marigolds are often preferred for their flavor in Europe and Russia, where they are an essential ingredient in spice mixtures containing garlic, chili pepper, and walnuts.

Nasturtiums: The aroma and taste of nasturtium leaves are rather peppery, akin to watercress, making them lovely choices for salads, garnishing quiches and omelets, or even a risotto. Associated with the fire element, use nasturtium flowers to invoke physical energy and protection.

Rose Petals: Long ago there were many recipes for using roses, as the Victorians loved the romance and magic of this erotic and elegant flower. To invoke love and passion, chop petals and stir with a little sugar into sliced strawberries, fresh raspberries, or chopped mango. Serve with fresh cream.

Violets and Violas: Delicate violets evoke a sweet and gentle response. In salads and desserts they impart both elegance and simple beauty. Garnish a cold soup, or place them atop a special cake. You are sure to invite appreciation and affection.

Herbal Oils, Vinegars, and Butters

One very simple way to bring magic to your fingertips is to create your own herbal oils, vinegars, and butters. With a little forethought and planning you'll have potent and flavorful potions ready and waiting for your next intention. To be magically spontaneous, it helps if you're well prepared!

Choose fresh herbs according to your intention and create potent aromatic oils that you can drizzle on everything from salad greens to cooked pasta, soups to roasted vegetables, fresh rustic bread to homemade pizza.

Herbal vinegars make salads extra special. Herbal butters will keep in the refrigerator for up to two weeks, and are wonderful to use in cooking or as appetizing magical spreads on your fresh breads and muffins.

Herbal Oils

Start with the best extra virgin olive oil you can afford, as there is a vast difference. Good olive oil not only has a superior flavor and silky consistency, it is far more stable, and does not turn rancid like so many other more volatile oils on the market today. Many food markets carry excellent Italian extra virgin olive oils in economy-sized tins, and they frequently offer sales.

You will need a clean sterile bottle with a cork; or try recycling bottles you may already have on hand. I use recycled vinegar and fancy olive oil bottles from gourmet gifts I've received. I buy pouring stoppers at a local cook shop (they fit most bottles), and with a small investment, I have a perfect vessel for my homemade herbal oil.

HERBAL OIL

Here is the basic recipe for making an herbal oil. Simply choose any single herb listed below, or a combination of herbs, to make your own magically inspired variations.

2 cups extra virgin olive oil

½ cup fresh herbs or 4 to 6 sprigs

The best herbs for infusing oils are basil leaves, bay leaves, dried chili peppers, garlic cloves (whole, peeled), lemon thyme, mint leaves, oregano, rosemary, savory, and thyme. Adding the spice of a few whole peppercorns, cumin seeds, coriander, or mustard or dill seeds gives the herbal oil added kick.

Place your herbs in a sterilized jar and pour the olive oil over the herbs. Cover and allow to stand for 2 to 3 weeks. Transfer the oil into a sterilized bottle, adding some of the herb sprigs if you desire, and enjoy!

Moonlit Kitchen Tip

If you're in a hurry for your herbal oil, you may gently heat the olive oil in a saucepan, and infuse the herbs for 5 to 10 minutes. Remove from heat and transfer the oil into a sterilized bottle. Store in a cool, dark place.

Herbal Vinegars

Add a dash of magic to your salads, roasted vegetables, marinades, and stir-fries with herbal in-fused vinegars. Wine, rice, sherry, or cider vinegars all have their own distinct character, and all are suitable for infusing.

HERBAL VINEGAR

Here is the basic recipe for an herbal vinegar.
Experiment with your own combination of flavors for culinary and magical purposes.

2 cups vinegar, red or white wine, apple cider, or brewed rice

2 cups fresh picked herbs, cleaned and patted dry

Favorable choices for vinegars include basil, borage, chives, cranberries, dill, garlic cloves, lavender, lemon balm, lemon thyme, mint, nasturtium flowers, rosemary, tarragon, thyme, and violets.

Briefly crush the herb leaves or sprigs to release their flavor and scent and place them in a glass jar. Pour in your vinegar of choice, cover, and place the jar in the sun. Flavors develop more quickly in the heat and sunlight, so check your infusion after a week. If you are storing the vinegar away from direct sun, the process could take up to 3 weeks. When the vinegar is ready, strain it and pour it into a sterilized bottle. Add a fresh herb sprig and a few peppercorns, coriander, or mustard seeds, then stop up the bottle and enjoy.

Herb Butters

Making herb butters is an easy and rewarding task. Herb butters are wonderful slathered on grilled fish, poultry, and roasted vegetables, or baked potatoes, rice, and pasta—not to mention a fresh slice of crusty bread still warm from the oven.

HERB BUTTER

Here is a basic recipe for making an herbal butter. Try your own combinations and delight in the fresh lively taste herbs bring to such a simple luxury. If you cannot eat real butter, try adding herbs to a good substitute. Some of the new margarines are quite tasty.

5 tablespoons chopped fresh herbs

1 cup (2 sticks) butter, softened

1 tablespoon fresh lemon juice

Herbs such as basil, red pepper flakes, chives, dill, lemon thyme, marjoram, mint, parsley, peppercorns, rosemary, tarragon, and thyme all bring their distinct nuance and magic to your table.

Combine the ingredients in a small bowl and blend well. Form the butter into a round shape, or ball, then wrap and refrigerate.

Moonlit Kitchen Tip

Using the recipe above, make a delicious spread by using your favorite cream cheese or Neufchâtel instead of butter—delightful on bagels, scones, muffins, and crackers.

LUNAR LESSONS AND MOONLIT MENUS

Cooking by moonlight is an intuitive approach to using the spiritual wisdom inherent in nature; it is about learning to trust one's instincts and tuning in to the underlying messages present in our daily life. Guidance is always available to us, if we learn to truly *listen*.

In the following monthly meditations, we will look toward the allegorical Wheel of the Year, reflect upon its annual pattern, and observe the monthly moon. Think of the earth as sacred and the moon as our mirror. Each new moon imparts a unique lesson for us to contemplate, a step in the cyclic dance of the lunar year. Every full moon offers us an opportunity to celebrate our gifts and manifest the fruition of our efforts.

In ritual cooking, your magical intentions become more potent if you work on issues aligned with the lessons of each changing moon. Offered at the end of each moon's meditation is an appropriate menu of recipes featuring seasonal foods to support your body and deepen your connection to the Goddess' supple guise. As you stir your culinary alchemy, work your intentions into these recipes and watch magic unfold. Follow now, in the footsteps of the Goddess, and delight in her monthly instruction.

We begin the year with the archetypal goddess about to enter her Maiden aspect as a pale fingernail crescent—a slim elegant curve of light that embodies the promise of the year's unfolding.

January: Month of the Snow Moon

During the long dark of a January night, the Aquarius new moon brings questions that quietly stir within our unknown self. As the darkness deepens we may feel impassive, observant, and watchful. It is a time to rest and surrender to the white goddess of the icy north. Her presence embodies silence. Her spirit is deep, rooted in the solid earth despite her aura of aloof detachment. We may feel a sense of isolation at this time. The rebirth of spring seems so far away. The truth of our purpose may seem hidden underground. Our connection to life and all living things may feel buried . . . but it is there.

The Aquarius new moon reminds us that it is our sacred duty to unearth our highest intentions, discover our inborn gifts, and open our eyes to the needs of community, while defining our own individuality.

As you ponder your deep-rooted purpose, pay close attention to your intuition. Let your dreams inform your waking life. Take time to simply *be* in the silence of winter. Nurture your body with plenty of rest and restore your energy with grounding foods. Celebrate the emerging crescent moon as she waxes to fullness. The Goddess as Maiden informs our newly found hopes and dreams. Perhaps your own idealistic dreams will begin to glimmer awake in the light of this snow moon.

Menu for the Snow Moon

Two-Cheese Fondue   73

Winter Pear-Apple-Butternut Soup   93

Olive and Rosemary-Raisin Focaccia   109

Savory Glazed Turkey "Meat Loaf"   126–127

Two Potato Gratin   147

Sun-Kissed Carrots Baked in Foil   148

Chocolate Mint Brownies   183

Hot Toddy   59

February: Month of the Quickening Moon

Our veiled Goddess emerges now as the tender bride this month of Imbolc, sparkling in her innocence and renewal. She is radiant, lovely, and perfect in her slender, deftly defined crescent. Our own energy begins to stir in anticipation of the promised spring. Snow drops have pushed through the frosted crust of winter to offer hope that new life is immanent.

The new moon in Pisces inspires the inner mystic and invites us to let go of control and give in to our deeper tidal energies. Rather than setting goals and intentions with conscious effort and focus, this new moon teaches us another path: the way of the mystic—fluid, receptive, and empathic. It is a time to honor our intuition and open ourselves to possibility, to yield to the Great Mystery, to loosen our collective grip on the external world and our functioning, striving, competing self. The distractions of our achievements can deafen our ears to the simple truths that the Goddess teaches us: that we are *all* an aspect of each other, interconnected, moving in opposites and creating the whole. The joy of Imbolc tickles our desire to an awareness of our counterpart. In anticipation, celebrate the quickening moon with foods befitting a bride adorned in eternal white.

Menu for the Quickening Moon

Pesto Artichoke Hearts Baked in Parmesan   74

White Bean Soup with Rosemary   94

Creamy Garlic Grits   149

Savory Muffins   110

Baked Chicken Breasts in Lemon Tarragon Cream   128–129

Lemon-Ginger Green Beans   150

Coconut-Whipped Winter Squash   151

Baked Croissant Pudding   184

Dream-Walker Tea   60

March: Month of the Sap Moon

The Goddess is now a Maiden, brightening with every lengthening day, as we approach the Spring Equinox, the moment of equal light and dark. Her crescent rises in the east, fuller now and beginning to ripen. The Green Man of the forest is rousing awake. His time is coming. Ostara marks the celebration of his coming rebirth, when daylight begins to increase and the green returns. For those of us who follow a path dedicated to the Goddess, this is a time of renewal and regeneration, a time of clearing away the lingering lessons of winter's long introspection and making way for new growth. We stir from the surrender of our Piscean dreams, turning now to our awakening bodies. Our energy begins to flow outward, extroverted in the stimulation of spring.

The new moon in Aries challenges us to look ahead with anticipation, asserting the power of "I am." Our center of attention shifts from our intuitive nature to our solar plexus, aptly named. This new moon provides us with an opportunity to create a focus for our goals, to honor spontaneity and take risks. This is the moment to be direct, leap into a new venture, risk a new project, or dare to make the first move. In the meantime, stir up some magic in the kitchen and wake up those taste buds.

Menu for the Sap Moon
Lemon Hummus 87

Crispy Sweet Potato Skins 85

Roasted Vegetable Chowder 95

Orange-Walnut Scones 111

Balsamic Roasted Chicken with Peppers 130–131

Karri Ann's Colcannon 152

Roasted Tomatoes Provencal 153

Lemon Pie with Raspberry Sauce 186

Irish Coffee 61

April: Month of the Budding Trees Moon

The Goddess calls us to dance this month. Make movement a part of this month's moon rituals. The body needs to stretch and reawaken this time of year. Play music that inspires you to move—ancient rhythms that resonate within your solar plexus. Be present in your body as you breathe and sway, opening yourself to rebirth and renewal. Embody the Goddess in this season of awakenings. Dance and revel in the mysteries of sensuality, the take and give of the feminine uniting with the masculine, of life generating new life.

Pleasure and desire are holy pursuits. Eve's apple was never a temptation to sin, it was an invitation to consciousness. In spring, the Goddess teaches us that the body and soul are one, each an integral part of the other. The soul expresses itself through the body, and the body breathes the very life of the soul. Both are sacred.

A Taurus new moon invites us to become children of nature, to live in the moment, secure in our place on earth. It is a time to be generous and gather loved ones close. Create comfort in your surroundings. Let the earthy nature of Taurus emerge and ground yourself with new roots that promise a harvest ahead. In this bright season of renewal, celebrate the awakening earth, welcome the Green Man, and honor the divine within you. Rekindle your passion, body and soul.

Menu for the Budding Tree Moon

Goddess Punch   62

Crab Melt Crostini   75

Lemony Chicken Caesar Salad   173

Gingery Carrot Soup   96

Maple-Nut Muffins   112

Grecian Quiche   132-133

Pasta Frittata   154

Asparagus Spears in Lemon Vinaigrette   155

Lemony Garlic Artichokes   156

Coconut Cake   188–189

May: Month of the Flower Moon

A favorite time for lovers of the Goddess, May 1 marks the birth of summer for many. Known as Beltane in Celtic lore, this cherished fire festival celebrates the power of the sun warming the earth into her season of fertility, evoking the union of the Goddess and God.

Our Goddess is truly astonishing as she approaches her full moon eminence. Hawthorne trees flower and violets bloom purple amidst lily of the valley. It is an exhilarating time filled with the fragrant enchantments of the season, a time for packing picnics and drinking wine beneath the stars. The lessons now are gentle ones. The urge to partner and find one's soul mate stirs even the most apathetic heart.

This month's new moon in Gemini brings a light touch to our lunar lessons. It is a time for communication, lively and sparkling, a time for opening one's self to possibility and allowing change to gust its breath of fresh air and clear away impeding doubts. Invite your hidden shadow self to come out and play in the moonlight. Awaken the child in you as you allow a sense of new wakefulness to rekindle your energy. Invite friends in for a party and celebrate.

Menu for the Flower Moon

Salmon and Sun-Dried Tomato Dip   88

Sherry-Walnut Goat Cheese Spread   89

Tomato Soup with a Lemon-Mint Swirl   97

Lemon Bread   113

Athena's Olive and Artichoke Chicken on Angel Hair Pasta   134–135

Spring Greens with Asparagus Tips and Oranges   174

Ginger-Frosted Pineapple Cake   185

Tahitian Goddess Smoothie   63

June: Month of the Strawberry Moon

The Oak King has leafed out his stately grandeur, and our Goddess is lush, ripe, and full. Mirrored as the moon, she is brilliant in her totality, round and immaculate. We have moved from the youthful Maiden aspect into the nurturing Mother, warmed by the southern sun. Midsummer night, also known as Litha, brings us the longest day of the year, warm and heady with evocative dreams and erotic whispers. This is the final moment of the sun's maximum power; for the remaining year he will slowly diminish, as the Wheel turns round in its ever-enduring cycle.

Celebrate your own full potential now. Realize that your dreams are awaiting the power of your focus and intention. The Goddess is fully abundant as Gaia, great Mother; she is generous and bountiful.

The new moon in Cancer brings us lessons of water, the symbol of our emotional being. Now is a good time to make room for contemplation and turn attention to your emotional life. Do you feel nurtured and cared for? Are your loved ones sensitive to the give and take of mutual support and receptivity? Take time to create the home life you desire. Fill your space with flowers and beauty. Revel in high season's abundance and let go of old outworn patterns. Remember that in order for you to truly receive, your hands must be open and empty.

Menu for the Strawberry Moon

Coconut Crab and Avocado Salad   76

Chilled Roasted Red Pepper Soup   98

Orange Tea Bread   114

Lemon Vegetable Penne with Pine Nuts   125

Herbed Fruit Salad   175

Maple Baked Beans   157

Strawberry Snow   187

Lemon Herb Cookies   190

Golden Midsummer Punch   65

July: Month of the Blessing Moon

By July the Goddess' moon has edged beyond completeness and begun to wane in her solar mirror. She is the mature Mother, the accomplished earthy woman with her roots deep in the land and a laugh hearty and welcoming. As Earth Mother, her agricultural abundance is given freely now, and we are in the thick of the first harvest. As we relax into the hot and sultry days of summer, we turn toward simple pleasures: walking barefoot, tending our herbs, swimming in moonlight, or drifting in the hammock. Our dreams are of gardening or fishing at the edge of deep, still water. There is no urgency that nudges us. Life feels complete.

The new moon lessons of fiery Leo are sun-filled and extroverted. It is a time to cultivate a center core of self-worth and entitlement, a time to nurture our inner fire, a time to deepen our courage and commitment to leadership, to take a stand and voice our creativity. Recognize your gifts and express them freely. Trust in the process of your intuition and behave generously. Look to the year's lessons and contemplate how you are reaping the outcome of seeds sown earlier in the year's Wheel. Is your harvest bearing fruit? Are your dreams well tended? Take time to share the summer's bounty and gather together friends for a backyard picnic. Fire up the grill in honor of the sun.

Menu for the Blessing Moon

Olive and Roasted Pepper Tapenade   77

Chilled Cucumber Soup   99

Summer Tomato Salad with Fresh Basil   176

Barbecued Fish in Foil Packets   138

Grilled Hot Potatoes   158

Cape Cod Bannock   119

Roasted Corn on the Grill   159

Raspberry-Peach Cobbler   191

Iced Irish Coffee   64

August: Month of the Corn Moon

By August our Goddess is spinning gold. The fields of corn have ripened to harvest, wheat is the color of amber, and chilies are being gathered for roasting. As the days shorten more noticeably and the evening's cool holds the hint of coming fall, our beautiful Goddess is deepening in her wisdom and inner beauty. Her waning crescent is more sharply defined, yet hangs without apology in the western sky. Her consort's power is lessening, but she bathes in his slanted light with joy. The harvest brings the time of sacrifice, when legendary John Barleycorn is cut down to offer his nourishment for the greater good of all. In Native American lore, the Corn Mother feeds her children with sacred food, the Three Sisters: corn, beans, and squash.

The new moon in Virgo brings lessons of duty, attention to detail, and sharpened instincts. It is a time to concentrate keenly on your goals and determine what is productive and what is wasteful. Is your energy and time invested wisely? Do you need to reexamine your priorities with an unerring eye and reset your intentions? This is the perfect time for symbolically separating the wheat from the chaff. And when you have clarified your vision, gather loved ones close to celebrate with Southwestern-inspired flavors.

Menu for the Corn Moon

Summer Berry Smoothie   66

Avocado and Roasted Red Pepper Quesadillas   78–79

Chilled Avocado Soup with Lime   100

Chili Cornbread   116

Crabmeat Enchiladas   136–137

Santa Fe Rice   160

Cantaloupe Salad with Coconut–Sour Cream Dressing   177

Spiced Squash and Maple Beans   161

Frozen Margarita Pie   192

September: Month of the Harvest Moon

As the second harvest arrives, our maturing Goddess reveals her first silver strands of wisdom. We gather the fruits of our labors and celebrate Mabon, the Autumnal Equinox, a bittersweet moment of balance in the year's Wheel, when day briefly equals night before darkness steadies its gain.

This month's moon hangs its sharpened dignity over burnished fields, her luminous shape lessening now as she wanes into the Crone's crescent. It is a time to scan the horizon and prepare for the coming cold. The Sun King is dying and the Goddess turns her mourning into shimmering beauty, deep and exquisite. As saddened as we are to let go of summer's abundance, there is a vitality that infuses us this cherished time of year, an urgency to savor each day and every last golden slant of warmth.

The new moon in Libra teaches us balance. Echoing the lessons of Mabon, she imparts her philosophy of fairness, equilibrium, and the aesthetics of poise. Take the time now to examine your life with an impartial eye, and readjust goals and efforts to reflect more balance in your life. In caring for others are you also fair to yourself? Are your priorities truly indicative of the whole of you? Think holistically about your choices and assess your inner and outer needs with a sense of self-reliance and impartiality. A willingness to share your garden's harvest is deepened when your own needs are met.

Menu for the Harvest Moon

October: Month of the Moon of the Falling Leaves

Our Goddess is now the wholly silvered Crone, the Wise One, the archetypal witch, able to step back from her role as nurturing Mother and allow winter's deft hand to strike the killer frost. The days are shortening, the nights are filling with shadows and whispers. It is a deliciously spooky time of year that thrills the child in all of us. As the Goddess' mirror, the western moon is at its last fingernail, a mere slip of an edge, disappearing fast. It is time to take the year's lessons to heart and face our inner world alone. The coming winter season brings a turn inward. With Persephone as our guide we descend into the underworld to confront our fears and hollow out our wisdom.

The new moon in Scorpio proves a perfect escort. Her energies feed our intuition and deepen our secrecy. Emotions may intensify and reveal powerful truths. Take this opportunity to develop your instinctive nature. Give in to your true passions and explore the mysteries that call to you. Honor your complexity and value your inner Shadow. Our Shadow has much to teach us if we learn from it and embrace it. Mark the Celtic New Year with favorite Halloween foods and celebrate Samhain by honoring your ancestors and remembering those who have passed on to the Summerland before you.

Menu for the Moon of the Falling Leaves

November: Month of the Dark Moon

The Goddess has gone underground, mourning her loss of the Sun King. The early evening sky deepens to blue-violet as the stars glitter their promise through darkened barren branches. Sunlight pales and fades earlier with each passing day. It is a time for taking stock and settling in for the long winter months ahead. Some of us with gypsy souls feel the urge to travel. The wanderer within looks to the horizon for friendlier climes. Geese pierce the air with their song of the dark moon, heading south in their geometric precision. It is a time for thanksgiving and for acknowledging the Mother's gifts.

The new moon in Sagittarius fuels our inner fire, as well as our restlessness with the status quo. It is a time for expression, giving voice to your philosophical self. Summon your enthusiasm for delving into your chosen path. Honor the seeker within you with exposure to new ideas, and feed your gypsy spirit with new philosophies to ponder. Books can be new roads to travel. Share yourself freely and honor the Goddess with your generosity. Gather together loved ones and rekindle friendship and affiliations, sharing the bounty of the recent harvest.

Menu for the Dark Moon

Sweet Potato Cakes with Lime Cream   84

Santa Fe Chicken Soup   103

Pumpkin Moon Bread   118

Roasted Onions, Portobello, and Goat Cheese on Pumpkin Polenta   142–143

Sesame-Crusted Sweet Potato Wedges   165

Braised Cabbage and Apples   166

Grapefruit and Spinach Salad   179

Pumpkin Cheesecake   194

Sun-Kissed Hot Chocolate   69

December: Month of the Long Night's Moon

As we approach the darkest night of the year, we are filled with both the certainty of winter's cold and the anticipation of the coming solstice. Our abundant Goddess has all but disappeared from us. Her evergreens remain to remind us that her life is eternal. As the days quickly shorten to the briefest day of the year, we prepare for the coming gladness, the Winter Solstice—the Wheel's turning point for the Sun King's return. We look forward to the rebirth of the Goddess as Mare, Star of the Sea, giving birth to the archetypal Divine Child, our hope embodied in her infant son. At the moment when we are at our darkest place in the year's Wheel, we collectively rejoice in the return of light.

The new moon in Capricorn gives us the tenacity to continue our winter journey. Her lessons impart those of discipline, determination, and a steadfast heart. This is the perfect time to focus on your hopes and dreams, setting goals for the future and constructing the foundation upon which to build your intentions into reality. Take advantage of the practicality of this moon and problem-solve. Know that you already possess all that you need to obtain what you seek. Find strength in the sun's gentle return, and celebrate the Goddess' guise as the eternal Divine Mother, whose love gives birth to light itself.

Menu for the Long Night's Moon

Blue Moon or Thirteenth Moon

Popular folklore about the concept of a blue moon has often shifted with the tides. After much research and debate the current thinking runs along two lines, the first being that a blue moon is the second full moon that occurs within one month. This association was popularized by an amateur astronomer in the 1940s. More recently, moon gazers have begun to wonder about a correlation based on the old *Maine Farmer's Almanac* that listed a blue moon as the third full moon occurring within a season of four moons. (Seasons usually contain only three.) While the true origin of blue moons remains a mystery, we can choose to celebrate a thirteenth moon for our own magical reasons. It's simply fun!

If a blue moon happens to occur, and they are rare, why not stir up some extra magic for the month and try something new? Take a risk with your creativity, step out of your usual mode of thinking, or break away from ingrained habits. Gather together friends and loved ones to celebrate the blue moon and create an innovative menu with foods you do not ordinarily cook. Light blue candles, play cool jazz, and wear something seductive . . . and blue, of course.

Menu for a Blue Moon

Avocado Mango Salsa   86

Cape Cod Tuna Salad   180

Three Sisters Stew   105

Blueberry Bread   121

Salmon-Scallion Cakes with Lime-Horseradish Mayonnaise   144

Garlicky Scalloped Potatoes   170

Blue Moon Berry Crisp   198

Dream-Walker Tea   60

Goddess-Worthy Beverages

As every wise woman knows, beverages work a special kind of magic. From cold weather warm-ups to festive punches, home-crafted libations add style and romance to gatherings both large and intimate. Sipping an herb-infused tea soothes the spirit as well as the body. Smoothies chock-full of immune-boosting vitamins energize us from the inside out. Celebrate each season's moon with a special brew, stirred with your magical intentions.

HOT TODDY

An old-fashioned libation to warm you up during the bone-chilling days of winter.
This is a favorite cure-all.

1 shot Scotch whiskey

1 tablespoon honey

1 bag Irish Breakfast Tea

Boiling water

Garnish

Fresh lemon slice

Prepare one mug per person as follows: Put 1 shot of Scotch, 1 tablespoon honey, and 1 tea bag in each mug. Pour in boiling hot water to fill, and steep for 1 to 2 minutes. Remove the tea bag, add a slice of lemon for garnish, and serve.

MAKES 1 HOT TODDY

DREAM-WALKER TEA

*Enhance your dreaming during the Piscean new moon with this herbal blend designed
to relax your body and stimulate your dreaming mind.*

¼ cup lavender buds

½ cup chamomile flowers

½ cup peppermint leaves

½ cup dried hops

3 star anise

2 cinnamon sticks, broken into
  pieces

1 teaspoon whole cloves

1 tablespoon orange peel

Honey (optional)

Blend all the ingredients together in a bowl and store in an airtight container or bag that zips. Before bedtime, bring a pot of fresh cold water to a boil, and steep 1 tablespoon of the mixture in 8 ounces of steaming, boiled water. Allow it to infuse for 5 minutes. Strain. Add a dab of honey if desired, and sip slowly.

Place your dream journal by your bed, and set your intentions to dream.

MAKES APPROXIMATELY 2 CUPS OF LOOSE TEA MIXTURE

IRISH COFFEE

Enjoy this classic recipe by the fire on a blustery night, or experiment with other liqueurs for variations of this theme. Add some good Irish tunes and an engaging yarn or two.

1 cup freshly brewed coffee

1 teaspoon granulated sugar

2 ounces Irish whiskey

Garnish

2 tablespoons whipped cream

Stir together the coffee and granulated sugar until the sugar is dissolved. Add the whiskey and stir.

Garnish with whipped cream.

Moonlit Kitchen Tip

Replace the whiskey with the smooth liqueur Drambuie to make a Highlander coffee. Originating on the Isle of Skye, Drambuie is crafted from whiskey, heather honey, herbs, and spices—a centuries-old recipe.

For an Irish Mist coffee, replace the whiskey with the Irish liqueur Irish Mist, also made from whiskey, heather honey, and herbs. For a Mexican twist, use Kahlua; for a Jamaican twist, Tia Maria.

SERVES 1

GODDESS PUNCH

Perfect for any celebration you can dream up,
*this **Goddess Punch** is truly best sipped by the silvery light of the moon.*

2 bottles brut champagne

1 cup fresh squeezed orange juice

1 cup cranberry juice

¼ cup fresh squeezed lemon juice

1 cup Curaçao or Cointreau

1 tablespoon angostura bitters

1 large bottle sparkling orange
    or lemon mineral water

Garnish

Fresh flowers (organic, unsprayed),
    such as nasturtiums, pansies,
    rose petals, or lemon balm leaves

Combine the champagne, orange juice, cranberry juice, lemon juice, Curaçao, angostura bitters, and mineral water in a large punch bowl and stir deosil (clockwise) with intentions of love and celebration. Chill with a large block of ice, or ice cubes made from cranberry juice (to avoid diluting the delicate flavors).

Float flowers or herb leaves on top for garnish, and serve immediately, with a joyful heart.

SERVES 15 TO 20, DEPENDING UPON THIRST

TAHITIAN GODDESS SMOOTHIE

When the warmer weather begins to stir feelings of desire,
nourish your body and soul with a delicious fruit smoothie.

1 banana

1 cup chopped mango or melon

¼ cup organic vanilla yogurt

½ cup pineapple or tangerine juice

4 ice cubes

Pinch of freshly grated nutmeg
  or cinnamon

Place the banana, mango, and yogurt into a blender, cover, and purée for 30 seconds. Add the juice, ice cubes, and nutmeg. Cover tightly, and pulse the blender on and off to break up the larger pieces of ice. Purée until the consistency is smooth.

Enjoy immediately, from your head down to your toes.

MAKES 1 GENEROUS SMOOTHIE

ICED IRISH COFFEE

In the warmer summer months serve this chilled version of an Irish classic.
Replace the ice cubes with a small scoop of vanilla ice cream and you have dessert in a glass:
an Irish coffee float.

4 cups freshly brewed hot coffee

1 cup heavy cream or half-and-half

4 teaspoons superfine granulated
    sugar

4 tablespoons whipped cream

Ice cubes

8 ounces Irish whiskey

Garnish

Whipped cream

Freshly grated nutmeg or
    cinnamon

Combine the hot coffee, cream, and granulated sugar; stir well to dissolve the sugar, then cover and chill thoroughly.

When you are ready to serve, spoon 1 tablespoon of whipped cream into each of the 4 glass mugs and divide the coffee mixture among them. Add 3 ice cubes and 2 ounces of whiskey to each glass.

Garnish each serving with whipped cream and a sprinkle of nutmeg or cinnamon.

Serve with Irish music.

Moonlit Kitchen Tip

Make a delightful Mexican variation with Kahlua and replace the ice with a scoop of coffee ice cream.

Serves 4

GOLDEN MIDSUMMER PUNCH

*Celebrate the Goddess and the Green Man under the strawberry moon
with this fitting libation.*

2 (750-milliliter) bottles champagne
or sparkling white wine

1 (750-milliliter) bottle white
Bordeaux table wine

4 cups (16 ounces) sparkling lemon
mineral water

Block of ice

¼ cup Grand Marnier

½ cup Cognac

¼ cup superfine granulated sugar

Garnish

1 cup strawberries, stemmed,
thinly sliced

Fresh mint leaves

Rose petals, washed, unsprayed

Chill the champagne, white wine, and sparkling water overnight.

To serve, place the ice in a large punch bowl. Stir together the Grand Marnier, Cognac, and granulated sugar with intentions of love and celebration. Invite abundance and joy. When the sugar is dissolved, pour the mixture over the ice. Add the champagne, wine, and sparkling water, and stir deosil (clockwise).

Garnish with the sliced strawberries, fresh mint leaves, and washed, unsprayed rose petals.

Serve immediately, with laughter and love.

SERVES ABOUT 25 TO 30, DEPENDING UPON THIRST

SUMMER BERRY SMOOTHIE

*Use your blender as a cauldron and whip up a love potion that will delight your lover
and nourish body and soul in the summer heat.*

1 cup fresh raspberries

1 cup stemmed, sliced strawberries

1 cup organic strawberry or
   blueberry yogurt

½ teaspoon pure vanilla extract

½ cup cranberry juice cocktail

6 ice cubes

Garnish
Mint sprigs

Place the berries, yogurt, and vanilla in a blender, cover, and pulse briefly to purée the berries. Add the juice and ice cubes, cover tightly, and pulse again to break up the larger pieces of ice. Purée with intentions of passion until the drink is a smooth and creamy consistency. Pour into stemmed glasses, and garnish with fresh mint.

Share with your lover, or simply yourself!

SERVES 2

SPICED CRANBERRY APPLE CIDER

Traditional mulled cider blushes with the addition of native grown cranberries.

1 quart apple cider

2 cups cranberry juice cocktail

1 cinnamon stick

13 whole cloves

1 small apple, washed, stemmed, cored, and sliced crosswise

Garnish
Cinnamon sticks

In a large saucepan combine the cider, cranberry juice, cinnamon stick, cloves, and apple slices. Gently simmer the mixture for 20 minutes. Strain the cider through a fine sieve into a heat-proof pitcher, or transfer to a warming crock for serving.

Serve the warm mulled cider in mugs and garnish with fresh cinnamon sticks, if desired.

SERVES 8

WASSAIL

This simple wassail omits the problematic eggs.
Celebrate the Winter King with this warming libation.

1 gallon fresh apple cider

1 (2-quart) carton fresh pineapple
   juice

1 cup strong Irish tea, brewed

1 cup brandy

1 cup dry sherry or Madeira wine

Place in a cheesecloth sack:

1 tablespoon whole cloves

1 tablespoon whole allspice

2 cinnamon sticks

Combine the apple cider, pineapple juice, tea, brandy, and sherry in a large pot; stir.

Place the cloves, allspice, and cinnamon sticks in a cheesecloth sack, tie, and place the sack in the pot. Gently simmer for 1 hour.

Wassail can be also be warmed in a large Crock-Pot or slow cooker for 4 to 6 hours, with the lid on.

SERVES 15 TO 20

SUN-KISSED HOT CHOCOLATE

Serve this delightful hot chocolate as a gift of love . . .
and make sure the guests kiss the cook!

4 cups organic milk

8 ounces semisweet chocolate chips
or bittersweet chocolate bar, cut
into pieces

5 2-inch strips (about ½ inch wide)
fresh orange peel (no white pith,
as it is bitter)

1 teaspoon instant espresso powder
or strong instant coffee

4 tablespoons granulated sugar

Freshly grated nutmeg

Garnish
Freshly grated nutmeg

Combine the milk, chocolate chips, orange peel, espresso powder, granulated sugar, and nutmeg (to taste) in a heavy-bottomed, medium saucepan. Stir constantly over low heat until the chocolate and the sugar melt. Increase the heat and bring the milk to steaming, stirring often.

Remove the pan from heat and, using a wire whisk, whip the cocoa until it is frothy. Return the pan to medium heat and bring to a near boil. Remove from heat, and whisk again until frothy. Discard the orange peel. Pour the hot chocolate into four mugs or glass Irish coffee mugs.

For garnish, grate extra nutmeg on top of the hot chocolate.

Serving Suggestion
Serve with a bowl of freshly popped popcorn.

SERVES 4

Appetizers, Dips, and Spreads

One of life's simple pleasures, appetizers bring people together, tease our taste buds, and start the conversation flowing. If you are entertaining, gather the fruits and flora of the season and decorate your edible offerings with nature's bounty. A simple display of fresh fruits, cut flowers, autumn leaves, or evergreens add a natural and creative touch. To add warmth and sensuality to your table, light vanilla, pumpkin, or cinnamon-scented candles.

TWO-CHEESE FONDUE

Fondue is a perfect midwinter treat: romantic, sensuous, and comforting all at once.
One amiable tradition insists that if a person accidentally drops her bread into the fondue
pot, she must immediately turn and kiss the person sitting on her left.
So position yourself at the table strategically!

½ pound natural Emmenthaler cheese, diced

½ pound natural Gruyère cheese, diced

2 tablespoons flour or cornstarch

1 garlic clove, peeled, halved

1 cup dry white wine

1 tablespoon lemon juice

1 tablespoon kirsch (cherry brandy)

Freshly grated nutmeg

Sea salt and freshly ground pepper

Dash of hot pepper sauce (optional)

2 loaves of crusty French bread, cut into bite-size pieces, with each retaining some crust

Garnish
Sweet pickles, pepperoncini, or roasted peppers

Place the cheeses in a bowl and dredge (coat) with flour. Rub the inside of the fondue pot with the cut sides of the garlic clove. Pour in the wine and lemon juice, and set the pot on low heat. Bring the liquid to a gentle simmer. Start adding the cheese gradually, stirring constantly with a wooden spoon until all the cheese is melted. (Melting the cheese slowly maintains a smooth fondue.) When the fondue is a velvet consistency, add the kirsch, nutmeg, sea salt, pepper, and hot pepper sauce. Continue to keep the fondue hot, but not bubbling. If the fondue begins to thicken, simply add a little more white wine to thin.

To serve the fondue, arrange the bread and bowls of pickles (or your choice of garnish) around the pot, and offer everyone a long fondue fork and plenty of napkins. Each person spears his own bread, through the crusted side, and dips it into the melted cheese. Let the swirling and dripping begin!

Serving Suggestion
Experiment with heavier dark breads such as pumpernickel and rye. You may also offer an assortment of sturdy steamed veggies (such as broccoli, cauliflower, or halved baby red potatoes), or even tart raw apple slices.

Moonlit Kitchen Tip
Traditionally, dipping foods and garnishes are served on a "lazy Susan," but placing serving plates and bowls around the pot will work just fine. To make this fondue wheat-free, simply substitute cornstarch for the flour.

SERVES 4 TO 6

PESTO ARTICHOKE HEARTS BAKED IN PARMESAN

Warm the cockles of your beloved's heart with this impressive (but so simple!)
hot appetizer featuring pesto made from basil, the love herb.
Wonderful accompanied with a goblet of Italian white wine.

2 (12-ounce) jars marinated
    artichoke hearts, drained well

2 tablespoons basil pesto

Dash of cayenne pepper

1 cup shredded Parmesan cheese

Extra virgin olive oil

Preheat the oven to 350 degrees.

Cut the artichoke hearts into bite-size pieces. In a mixing bowl, toss the artichokes with the pesto until they are coated. Lightly season with a little cayenne pepper to taste.

Pour the artichokes into a lightly oiled oval baking dish. Sprinkle with the Parmesan, and drizzle extra virgin olive oil over the top. Bake for about 15 minutes, or until the artichokes are heated through and the cheese is nicely melted.

Serving Suggestion

Serve with thin crostini (toasted slices of French baguette) or gourmet crackers.

SERVES 6 TO 8

CRAB MELT CROSTINI

A sensuous melting treat to offer friends and family when gathered for any celebratory feast.

1 pound lump crabmeat, picked over

½ cup light sour cream or nondairy sour cream

2 to 3 tablespoons mayonnaise

¼ cup chopped scallions or red onion

1 cup shredded cheese, Italian blend (asiago, provolone, Parmesan, mozzarella)

1 garlic clove, peeled, minced

⅛ teaspoon cayenne pepper, or to taste

½ teaspoon Old Bay Seasoning

1 French baguette, sliced fairly thin and lightly toasted

Garnish
Fresh parsley or mint, finely chopped

Preheat the oven to broil.

In a medium mixing bowl combine the crabmeat, sour cream, mayonnaise, scallions, shredded Italian blend cheeses, garlic, cayenne, and Old Bay Seasoning.

Place the bread slices on a large baking sheet, and lightly broil them, 5 to 6 inches from the heat, until toasted, about 1 to 2 minutes. Turn the bread slices over, and top each with about 1 tablespoon of the crabmeat mixture.

Continue to broil 5 to 6 inches from the heat until the cheese is melted and bubbly, about 2 to 3 minutes. Transfer the crostini (the toasted slices of French baguette) to a serving platter.

For garnish, sprinkle all the slices with parsley.

Serve immediately.

Moonlit Kitchen Tip
This delectable crab dish can be easily infused with herbs of intention. Just remember to taste test.

SERVES 6 TO 8

COCONUT CRAB AND AVOCADO SALAD

Delightfully light on a warm summer's eve, this seductive salad is a perfect food for love.

1 pound lump crabmeat, picked over

3 tablespoons fresh lime juice

¼ cup unsweetened coconut milk, well stirred

1 tablespoon light sour cream or mayonnaise

1 teaspoon sherry or balsamic vinegar

1 teaspoon red pepper flakes, for heat (optional)

¼ cup fresh cilantro, minced

Sea salt and freshly ground pepper

2 ripe avocados

4 scallions, chopped

Garnish
Fresh cilantro sprigs

Place the flaked crabmeat in a bowl.

In a separate bowl whisk together the lime juice, coconut milk, sour cream, sherry, red pepper flakes, and cilantro. Season to taste with sea salt and freshly ground pepper. Stir in the crab and mix well. If not assembling the salad right away, store the crab mixture in a covered container and chill.

When ready to serve, peel, pit, and slice the avocados. Divide the slices among four salad plates, and arrange the slices in a fan pattern. Spoon ¼ of the crab mixture onto each plate. Sprinkle with the chopped scallions and garnish with sprigs of fresh cilantro.

Serving Suggestion
Serve with a basket of lime-flavored tortilla chips.

SERVES 4

OLIVE AND ROASTED PEPPER TAPENADE

Classic French goddesses love to make their tapenade from black olives and anchovies.
My version is a less intense yet appetizing spread of green olives, roasted red peppers, garlic,
and pine nuts. Perfect for topping toasted slices of French bread or even crispy bagel chips.

2 cups green olives (drained if in brine), pitted and chopped

2 tablespoons chopped roasted red peppers (jarred is fine), well drained

2 garlic cloves, peeled

2 tablespoons pine nuts

¼ cup extra virgin olive oil

Fresh lemon juice squeezed from ½ lemon

Pinch of salt and cayenne pepper

Combine the olives, roasted peppers, garlic, and pine nuts in a food processor work bowl and purée until smooth. Slowly add the olive oil while the machine is running and process until the olive mixture is a smooth paste. Stop and scrape down the sides of the work bowl if necessary. Stir in the lemon juice, salt, and cayenne pepper. Transfer the tapenade to a serving bowl to enjoy immediately, or cover and refrigerate. Tapenade can be made in advance and stored in the refrigerator for up to five days.

Serving Suggestion
Serve with plenty of toasted French bread slices, gourmet crackers, or bagel chips.

Moonlit Kitchen Tip
Keep tapenade as a staple in your refrigerator and make almost instant meals. Spread it on pizza shells, toss it with hot pasta, or combine it with cream cheese for a lovely omelet.

Serves 4 to 6

AVOCADO AND ROASTED
RED PEPPER QUESADILLAS

Quesadillas are fairly simple to put together.
Cut into wedges, they make an appetizing start to any meal.
Try your own combinations and get creative in the kitchen!

1 large avocado (ripe, yet firm)

1 cup loosely packed roasted
    peppers, drained, chopped

2 tablespoons chopped red onion

2 teaspoons fresh lemon juice

1 teaspoon balsamic vinegar

½ teaspoon red pepper flakes,
    or to taste

¼ teaspoon ground cumin

1 tablespoon chopped fresh cilantro
    or parsley

Sea salt and freshly ground pepper

4 medium fajita-size flour tortillas

1 tablespoon olive oil

1 cup crumbled chèvre (goat
    cheese), or grated Monterey
    Jack cheese

Preheat a flat griddle to 350 degrees, or heat a large nonstick frying pan on medium heat.

Remove the pit from the avocado, slice the avocado into quarters, and peel. Dice the avocado and place in a small bowl with the roasted peppers, onion, lemon juice, balsamic vinegar, red pepper flakes, cumin, and cilantro. Season with sea salt and freshly ground pepper to taste. Gently toss to mix the ingredients.

Brush the tortillas lightly with olive oil. Spread the avocado-roasted pepper mixture evenly over 2 of the tortillas, sprinkle the tortillas with the chèvre, and place the remaining 2 tortillas on top of each, pressing gently. Cook the quesadillas until they are just slightly browned, press down with a spatula, then gently flip them over. Cook on the remaining side until browned and melted. If doubling this recipe for more guests, the finished quesadillas may be kept warm on a baking sheet in a 200 degree oven.

When ready to serve, transfer quesadillas to a cutting board and cut each into 4 wedges. A pizza cutter works perfectly for this! Serve on a festive plate, each wedge garnished with a spoonful of sour cream and a cilantro sprig.

Garnish

Light sour cream or nondairy
sour cream

Cilantro sprigs

Moonlit Kitchen Tip

Quesadillas make an easy supper when you use whatever you happen to have on hand. Try leftover cooked chicken pieces topped with salsa and Monterey Jack cheese, or sautéed onions and mushrooms with cheddar cheese. The combinations are endless!

SERVES 4 AS AN APPETIZER,
OR 2 AS A LIGHT BRUNCH

MELTED GOAT CHEESE AND
BALSAMIC PEPPERS WITH CROSTINI

A simple combination of two Mediterranean favorites—
goat cheese and roasted peppers—makes an easy, delicious appetizer.

8 ounces chèvre (goat cheese)

Sea salt and freshly ground pepper

¾ cup jarred Italian roasted pepper salad, drained

1 teaspoon balsamic vinegar

1 French baguette, sliced thin, lightly toasted, or gourmet crackers

Preheat the oven to 325 degrees.

Soften the chèvre a little bit with a spoon and spread it into a small ovenproof baking/serving dish. Season with salt and pepper. Layer the Italian roasted pepper salad all over the top of the cheese, and sprinkle with balsamic vinegar. Bake just until the cheese is warmed and beginning to melt a bit, about 10 to 15 minutes.

In the meantime, cut the baguette into thin slices and toast lightly. Place the pieces in a basket.

Serve the melted goat cheese and balsamic peppers while still hot from the oven with the basket of crostini (the toasted slices of French baguette) or your favorite gourmet crackers.

Moonlit Kitchen Tip

In a pinch, substitute firm cream cheese for goat cheese.

SERVES 4

A SIMPLE GODDESS PIZZA

Sometimes the best things in life are the simplest.
This easy appetizer is a family favorite. It's also perfect for a light brunch.

1 large pizza shell or Italian
   flatbread, such as Boboli

1 cup prepared basil pesto

2 to 3 ripe juicy tomatoes, washed
   and sliced

1 (4-ounce) package of chèvre or
   Montrachet, sliced or crumbled

Extra virgin olive oil

Sea salt and freshly ground pepper

Garnish

Fresh basil leaves, chiffonade (roll
   the basil leaves together in a
   tight cigarlike shape and cross-
   cut the roll into thin strips)

Preheat the oven to 400 degrees.

Place your pizza shell on a pizza pan or baking sheet. Spread the pesto all over the surface of the shell. Arrange the tomato slices on the pesto. Add the slices of chèvre. Drizzle olive oil over the pizza, and season with sea salt and freshly ground pepper to taste. Bake for 7 to 10 minutes, until the cheese is melted and the crust is golden brown. Allow the pizza to set for 1 or 2 minutes before cutting.

Slice into small squares and serve with fresh basil leaves on top for garnish. Heavenly!

Moonlit Kitchen Tip

Make a Celtic-inspired pizza with thinly sliced cooked baby red or gold potatoes, sautéed onions, garlic, and pesto. Add appropriate herbs of intention and you've created a magickal moon pizza!

SERVES 4 TO 6 AS AN APPETIZER,
OR 2 AS A MAIN COURSE

CRAB CAKES WITH CRANBERRY-ORANGE SALSA

Crab cakes are always a special treat—
the perfect appetizer for a waxing or full moon celebration, in any season.

1 pound lump crabmeat, picked over

1 cup Italian-style seasoned bread crumbs

Sea salt and freshly ground pepper

Dash of cayenne pepper

2 large free-range eggs

⅓ cup mayonnaise

2 teaspoons Worcestershire sauce

1 tablespoon finely chopped scallions (white part only)

2 to 3 tablespoons canola or vegetable oil

Garnish
Cranberry Orange Salsa
Fresh lime wedges

In a mixing bowl gently combine the crabmeat and bread crumbs. Season with salt, black pepper, and cayenne pepper to taste. In a small bowl, whisk together the eggs, mayonnaise, Worcestershire sauce, and scallions, and add to the crab, tossing lightly with a fork, only until the crab mixture is evenly moistened.

Lay out a sheet of waxed paper to set the cakes on, and divide the mixture to form 8 round crab cakes.

In a large, heavy-bottomed skillet, heat the oil over moderate heat and fry the crab cakes until they are golden brown, about 4 minutes on each side. Drain briefly on a paper towel.

Garnish with a spoonful of the *Cranberry Orange Salsa* and a wedge of lime. Serve the crab cakes warm.

Cranberry Orange Salsa

12 ounces fresh cranberries

2 oranges, peeled, pith removed

3 garlic cloves, peeled

1 red bell pepper, seeded, cored, quartered

1 red onion, peeled, quartered

1 teaspoon ground cumin

1 jalapeno or poblano chili, seeded, stemmed

Dash of cayenne pepper

½ cup fresh cilantro, stems removed

2 tablespoons light brown sugar or honey

Juice from 1 fresh lime

Sea salt

Cranberry Orange Salsa

Process (or finely chop) the cranberries and place them in a mixing bowl. Process (or finely chop) the oranges, and add to the cranberries. Place the garlic, red bell pepper, onion, cumin, jalapeno, and cayenne in the food processor, and pulse/process (finely chop) for 1 minute. Add the cilantro, brown sugar, and lime juice, and continue to pulse/process until the cilantro is finely chopped. Stir this mixture into the cranberries and mix well. Season to taste with sea salt. Cover and chill until you are ready to serve.

Serving Suggestion

Serve the crab cakes on a bed of mesclun salad greens. You can also serve the *Cranberry Orange Salsa* with a basket of tortilla chips.

Moonlit Kitchen Tip

During cranberry season, stock your freezer with bags of fresh cranberries to have on hand through many moons.

SERVES 4

SWEET POTATO CAKES WITH LIME CREAM

Golden and savory, these cakes are a treat for any season of the moon.

3 medium sweet potatoes, peeled
    and grated

1 small onion, peeled, grated

1 large free-range egg, beaten with
    1 tablespoon milk

2 tablespoons unbleached all-
    purpose flour

Dash of freshly grated nutmeg

Sea salt and freshly ground pepper

Lime Cream

1 cup light sour cream or nondairy
    sour cream

2 tablespoons fresh lime juice

1 teaspoon light brown sugar

Sea salt and freshly ground pepper

Garnish

Fresh chives, finely chopped, or
    cilantro sprigs

Combine the potatoes and onion with the egg and milk mixture, and toss well to coat. Add the flour and season with nutmeg, sea salt, and pepper. Mix well.

Preheat a large nonstick skillet or griddle, and lightly coat with oil. Drop the potato batter by tablespoonfuls onto the heated surface and press down gently with a spatula to flatten slightly. Cook for 4 to 5 minutes on each side, until the cakes are cooked through and lightly crispy. Keep the first batch warm in a 300 degree oven while you make the remaining cakes and the *Lime Cream*.

Serve these savory cakes as appetizers with a spoonful of *Lime Cream* on the side. Garnish with chopped fresh chives or cilantro sprigs.

Lime Cream

Whisk the sour cream, lime juice, brown sugar, sea salt, and ground pepper together (or use a blender); mix well.

SERVES 4 TO 6 AS AN APPETIZER

CRISPY SWEET POTATO SKINS

Celebrate the full moon and the new moon with this savory snack, a family favorite.

2 medium-large sweet potatoes, scrubbed

Olive oil

1 teaspoon lemon pepper

½ teaspoon chili powder

4 tablespoons freshly grated Parmesan cheese

Garnish
Sour cream
Bacon bits

Preheat the oven to 400 degrees.

Cut the potatoes in half, lengthwise, and rub olive oil over them. Place on a baking sheet and roast for 45 minutes, until tender but firm. Remove from the oven and set aside to cool.

Scoop most (but not all) of the potato flesh out of the skins, leaving a ¼-inch shell. Place the potato skins back on the baking sheet and, using a large spatula, gently press down on the skins to flatten.

In a small bowl mix the lemon pepper, chili powder, and Parmesan cheese together. Sprinkle the mixture over the skins. Bake the skins for 10 minutes, until crispy.

Divide the skins into 4 servings, and offer sour cream and bacon bits for topping.

SERVES 4

Moonlit Kitchen Tip
Keep the sweet potatoes that you scooped out and use them for a quick side dish the next day. Just reheat and mash gently, adding butter and nutmeg. This recipe also works well with regular baking potatoes.

AVOCADO MANGO SALSA

This lively salsa makes any moon gathering festive. No mangoes?
Use local fruit in season, such as pears, peaches, or nectarines.
Serve with blue corn chips or as a side dish accompanying fish or spicy dishes.

1 mango, peeled, pitted, chopped

1 avocado (firm, yet ripe), peeled, pitted, and chopped

⅔ cup finely chopped red onion

½ cup finely chopped red bell pepper

1 garlic clove, peeled, minced

2 tablespoons fresh lime juice

1 teaspoon lime zest

1 tablespoon extra virgin olive oil

¼ cup chopped fresh cilantro or mint

Sea salt and freshly ground pepper

Combine all of the ingredients in a bowl and toss well. Taste for seasoning adjustments. Cover and chill. This salsa can be made up to 6 hours ahead of serving time.

Moonlit Kitchen Tip

For even more heat, add ½ teaspoon red pepper flakes. Fruit salsas are refreshing accompaniments to fish, poultry, egg, and curry dishes.

MAKES ABOUT 2 TO 3 CUPS

LEMON HUMMUS

This light and tangy version of the classic chickpea hummus is perfect
for waking up your taste buds after a long winter.

4 to 6 large garlic cloves, peeled

2 tablespoons extra virgin olive oil

2 tablespoons organic, plain, nonfat yogurt

1 (15-ounce) can garbanzo beans (chickpeas), drained

Juice of 1 fresh lemon

1 teaspoon ground cumin, or to taste

Sea salt

Cayenne pepper

Garnish

Fresh cilantro sprigs or chopped fresh parsley

Sprinkle of cayenne pepper or paprika

Swirl of extra virgin olive oil

In a food processor, mince the garlic. Add the olive oil and yogurt, and pulse to blend. Add the garbanzo beans, lemon juice, and cumin, and process until the mixture becomes a purée, occasionally scraping down the sides of the work bowl. Season the hummus to taste with sea salt and cayenne pepper. Transfer to a storage container, cover, and refrigerate. This hummus will keep well for 2 to 3 days.

Place in a serving bowl and garnish with a sprinkle of fresh cilantro sprigs, cayenne pepper, and a swirl of olive oil.

Serving Suggestion

Surround the bowl with crisp carrot sticks, celery, and broccoli florets, or slice some fresh pita bread into triangles, if desired.

Moonlit Kitchen Tip

Hummus makes a wonderful sandwich filling for pita breads, roll-ups, and rustic breads. Add some sprouts, grated carrot, sliced red onion, and cucumber, and you have a perfect waning moon sandwich. Add fresh juicy tomato wedges, a spoonful of rinsed capers, extra garlic, and fresh chopped mint, and you have a perfect love food!

SERVES 4 TO 6

SALMON AND SUN-DRIED TOMATO DIP

A delicious and different appetizer, perfect with a glass of wine and good conversation.

1 (14-ounce) can pink salmon, drained, picked over, flaked with a fork

1 (8-ounce) container whipped cream cheese

¼ cup light sour cream

¼ cup oil packed sun-dried tomatoes, drained well and chopped

2 tablespoons capers, drained and rinsed

1 tablespoon fresh lemon juice

1 tablespoon prepared horseradish, or to taste

2 teaspoons dried dill, or 1 tablespoon fresh

Dash of cayenne pepper

Sea salt and freshly ground pepper

Garnish
2 tablespoons fresh mint leaves, chopped

Combine all of the ingredients in a bowl and mix well. Cover and chill for 2 to 3 hours to allow the flavors to develop. Taste test for seasoning adjustments and garnish with the fresh mint.

Serving Suggestion
Serve the dip with crunchy bagel chips, pita bread toasts, or crostini.

Moonlit Kitchen Tip
Salmon is also available in vacuum-packed pouches, offering superior texture and flavor.

SERVES 6 TO 8

SHERRY-WALNUT GOAT CHEESE SPREAD

This versatile spread is wonderful to whip up for those heady days of May,
when guests may be dropping by to share a walk around the garden.

8 ounces soft chèvre

1½ tablespoons dry sherry or port

½ cup chopped walnuts or pecans

1 tablespoon chopped fresh parsley

1 tablespoon finely chopped chives

Fine sea salt and freshly ground
    pepper

In a food processor combine the chèvre and sherry, and process until it is smooth. Transfer to a bowl, and fold in the chopped walnuts, parsley, and chives. Blend well. Season with sea salt and freshly ground pepper to taste. Store in a covered container and chill.

Serving Suggestion
Serve with garlicky bagel chips, or your favorite gourmet crackers.

Moonlit Kitchen Tip
For a variation of this theme, try substituting blue cheese or cream cheese for goat cheese.

SERVES 4

Soulful Soups for Body, Mind, and Spirit

Simmering a homemade soup on the stovetop can conjure any magical intention your goddess self desires. Stir your soup deosil (clockwise) as you add seasonings appropriate for creating warmth, healing, friendship, nurturing, and reconciliation. Soups impart a primal satisfaction that feeds us on many levels. Stir up a little magic in your soup pot tonight, and fill your home with love.

WINTER PEAR-APPLE-BUTTERNUT SOUP

*Warm up the hearth with a fragrant simmering soup that will delight your senses,
comfort your body, and soothe your soul.*

2 tablespoons olive oil

1 sweet onion, peeled, diced

2 garlic cloves, peeled, minced

2 pounds butternut squash,
   peeled and diced

2 ripe Bartlett pears, peeled,
   seeded, cored, and chopped

2 Granny Smith apples, peeled,
   seeded, cored, and chopped

1 tablespoon mild curry powder

1 tablespoon light brown sugar or
   real maple syrup

Dash of dry sherry or vermouth
   (optional)

6 cups low sodium organic chicken
   broth or light vegetable broth

Sea salt and freshly ground pepper

1 cup half-and-half or coconut milk

Garnish
Sour cream or nondairy sour cream

Grated apple

Freshly grated nutmeg

In a heavy-bottomed soup pot, heat the olive oil over medium heat, add the onion, and cook gently, stirring frequently until the onion is softened, about 5 minutes. Add the garlic, squash, pears, apples, curry powder, and brown sugar, and sauté for 10 minutes. Add the sherry, if desired, and stir for 1 minute. Add the broth and season to taste with sea salt and ground pepper. Bring to a gentle boil. Reduce the heat and simmer, covered, until the squash and fruit are tender, about 20 minutes.

Purée the soup carefully with an immersion blender (or in batches, covered, in a blender or food processor).

Return the purée to the pot, and add the half-and-half. Gently warm through, being careful not to boil.

Serve in festive bowls and garnish each serving with a swirl of sour cream, a teaspoon of grated apple, and some freshly grated nutmeg.

SERVES 6

WHITE BEAN SOUP WITH ROSEMARY

An elegant yet hearty soup to nurture your winter weary soul. Serve with a basket of
warmed crusty bread for a light but nourishing waning moon supper.

2 tablespoons olive oil

1 yellow onion, peeled, diced

2 celery stalks, trimmed and
chopped

5 garlic cloves, peeled, minced

⅓ cup white wine

3 (1-pound) cans white cannellini
beans, drained, rinsed

2 medium Yukon Gold or white
potatoes, peeled and diced

5 to 6 cups organic chicken or
vegetable broth

2 teaspoons fresh rosemary leaves,
chopped

Sea salt and freshly ground pepper

1 cup baby spinach leaves or
escarole, washed

¼ cup freshly squeezed lemon juice

½ cup chopped fresh Italian parsley

Garnish

Extra virgin olive oil

Freshly grated Parmigiano-
Reggiano or good Parmesan

Heat the olive oil in a heavy-bottomed soup pot, add the onion and celery, then stir and sauté for about 5 minutes, until the onion is softened. Add the garlic and stir briefly (keep the garlic from browning). Add the wine and 1½ cans of the white beans, and mash lightly with a potato masher. Add the remaining white beans, the diced potatoes, and the broth. Add the rosemary, sea salt, and pepper to taste, then stir and bring to a simmer, cooking the soup for about 10 minutes. Add the spinach and lemon juice, cover, and simmer for 5 minutes. Uncover and add the parsley right before serving. Taste and adjust the seasoning.

Ladle into bowls. For garnish, drizzle extra virgin olive oil on top and pass around the freshly grated Parmigiano-Reggiano.

Serving Suggestion

Serve the soup with a basket of warm rustic bread.

Moonlit Kitchen Tip

To make this Tuscan-inspired soup into a hearty meal, add sliced cooked sausages (Italian, turkey, chicken, or veggie all work well).

SERVES 4 AS A MAIN COURSE,
OR 6 AS AN APPETIZER

ROASTED VEGETABLE CHOWDER

A richly flavored soup that's sure to warm you up during spring's damp and stormy season.

1 sweet onion, peeled, diced

1 pound baby red potatoes, scrubbed and sliced

2 large carrots, scrubbed and sliced

2 parsnips, peeled and sliced

2 tablespoons olive oil

5 garlic cloves, peeled, minced

1 teaspoon fennel seeds

½ teaspoon dried thyme

½ teaspoon dried marjoram

Sea salt and freshly ground pepper

1 quart organic chicken or vegetable broth

1 cup frozen corn kernels

1 cup half-and-half or light cream

3 tablespoons dry sherry (optional)

Preheat the oven to 375 degrees.

Combine the onion, potatoes, carrots, and parsnips in a roasting pan and toss with the olive oil, garlic, fennel seed, thyme, and marjoram. Season with sea salt and pepper. Roast the vegetables in the oven for about 50 to 60 minutes, until they are tender. Pour the broth into a soup pot and bring to a high simmer. Add the roasted vegetables, with all the bits and pieces from the pan. Add the frozen corn kernels. Cover and simmer for about 7 minutes. Add the half-and-half, stir and taste for seasoning adjustments, and warm through gently. Be careful not to boil the chowder once you've added the half-and-half. Add the sherry, if desired.

Serving Suggestion

Serve in deep bowls with a basket of warm crusty rye bread or hot buttered corn tortillas.

SERVES 4 AS A MAIN COURSE,
OR 6 AS AN APPETIZER

GINGERY CARROT SOUP

*Crocus and daffodils dot the April landscape with color. Stir up a pot of this sunny orange
soup to honor the hare moon, the bringer of warmth and awakenings.*

2 tablespoons olive oil

2 pounds baby carrots, washed

2 inches of fresh ginger, peeled and
   grated

1 teaspoon ground cumin

2 teaspoons light brown sugar

4 cups organic chicken or light
   vegetable broth

1 tablespoon fresh lemon or lime
   juice

1 (14-ounce) can coconut milk,
   well stirred

Sea salt and freshly ground pepper

Garnish

Carrot, grated

Fresh dill, mint, or cilantro,
   chopped

In a heavy soup pot heat the olive oil over medium heat. Add the carrots, ginger, and cumin, and cook and stir for about 3 minutes. Add the brown sugar and stir for about 3 minutes, until it caramelizes. Add the chicken broth and lemon juice, and bring to a boil. Reduce the heat to medium-low, cover, and simmer, stirring occasionally, until the carrots are tender, about 20 minutes. Purée the soup with an immersion blender until smooth (or purée the soup in batches, covered, in a food processor or blender and return to the pot). Add the coconut milk and season with sea salt and pepper to taste. Warm the soup on medium-low heat, taking care not to boil it. Stir occasionally, until heated through, about 3 to 4 minutes.

Serve immediately and garnish with freshly grated carrot, or dill, mint, or cilantro.

Moonlit Kitchen Tip

For a refreshing version of this soup, substitute fresh orange juice for the coconut milk.

Serves 4 to 6

TOMATO SOUP WITH A LEMON-MINT SWIRL

When spring fever turns our thoughts to love,
delight your partner with this fresh-tasting soup. Aphrodite would ardently approve!

2 tablespoons olive oil

1 red onion, finely chopped, reserve 2 tablespoons

2 garlic cloves, peeled, minced

½ teaspoon dried Italian herbs

½ teaspoon red pepper flakes

1 (28-ounce) can whole Italian tomatoes

Dash of sea salt

1 teaspoon granulated sugar

2 cups organic chicken or vegetable broth

1 bay leaf

Freshly ground pepper

½ cup organic, plain yogurt

2 teaspoons fresh mint, minced

2 teaspoons finely grated lemon zest

Garnish

Chopped mint

In a heavy soup pot heat the olive oil over medium heat. Add the onion and garlic and stir for 3 minutes. Add the Italian herbs and red pepper flakes, and stir for 1 to 2 minutes, until the onion is softened. Add the tomatoes, sea salt, and the granulated sugar. Pour the broth into the mixture. Add the bay leaf and season with pepper to taste. Cover and bring to a simmer. Lower the heat and continue to simmer for about 30 minutes.

In the meantime, combine the yogurt with the fresh mint and lemon zest in a small bowl; set aside.

Discard the bay leaf. Purée the soup with an immersion blender (or in small batches, covered, in a food processor or blender), and return to the pot. Add the 2 tablespoons of reserved onion. Taste for seasoning adjustments. Keep warm until serving.

To serve, ladle the soup into shallow bowls and swirl a spoonful of the yogurt mixture into the center of the soup. Drag a toothpick through the yogurt in a circular motion to create more of a spiral. Sprinkle with a little extra chopped mint.

Moonlit Kitchen Tip

For a change of pace, make pesto croutons. Toast a small slice of French bread for each serving, spread with your favorite pesto, and float in each bowl of soup.

Serves 4 as an appetizer

CHILLED ROASTED RED PEPPER SOUP

A zesty and vibrant cold soup, different from the usual gazpacho.

1 (15-ounce) jar of Italian roasted red peppers, drained

1 (14-ounce) can coconut milk, well stirred

2 cups organic, plain yogurt

1 tablespoon fresh lime juice

1 teaspoon red pepper flakes, or to taste

2 tablespoons chopped fresh basil

Sea salt and freshly ground pepper

Garnish

2 to 3 tablespoons finely chopped red onion

2 to 3 tablespoons chopped fresh mint or basil

In a food processor or blender, purée the peppers with the coconut milk. Add the yogurt, lime juice, pepper flakes, basil, sea salt, and pepper, and purée until smooth and creamy. Taste for seasoning adjustments. Store in a covered container and chill for at least 1 hour.

Spoon into chilled bowls and garnish with a small spoonful of chopped red onion and a pinch of mint or basil.

Serving Suggestion

Serve with blue corn tortilla chips or crispy rice crackers.

SERVES 6

CHILLED CUCUMBER SOUP

Keep your cool with this lively creamy appetizer. Make this perfect summer soup at least 6 to 8 hours before eating and chill in the fridge until you are ready to serve it.

4 cucumbers, peeled, seeded, and chopped, plus 1 additional cucumber, peeled and diced fine

1 cup organic, plain yogurt or light sour cream

1 (14-ounce) can coconut milk, well stirred

¼ teaspoon ground cumin

Sea salt and freshly ground pepper

2 tablespoons fresh mint leaves, chopped

1 tablespoon fresh dill, chopped

Garnish

Cucumber slices

Fresh herbs such as mint, dill, or chives, chopped

In a blender or food processor purée the 4 cucumbers with the yogurt, coconut milk, cumin, sea salt, and pepper to taste. Transfer the purée to a storage bowl. Cover and chill the soup at for least 6 hours, even overnight.

When you are ready to serve the soup, add the remaining cucumber, the mint leaves, and the fresh dill.

Spoon into chilled serving bowls and garnish each with 3 thin cucumber slices and either mint, dill, or chives.

SERVES 4

CHILLED AVOCADO SOUP WITH LIME

A smooth and creamy beginning to any summer meal,
this soup is delightful when the weather is sultry.

2 ripe avocados, peeled, pit
   removed, quartered

1 cup organic, plain yogurt

2 cups chilled light vegetable broth

2 tablespoons fresh lime juice

1 chili pepper (as hot as you like),
   seeded, finely diced

Sea salt and freshly ground pepper

Garnish
Thin lime slices

2 tablespoons fresh mint, chopped

In a blender or food processor, purée the avocado with the yogurt, chilled broth, lime juice, and chili pepper, until it is smooth and creamy. Season to taste with sea salt and pepper, and chill in a covered container for at least 2 hours.

Serve in chilled bowls topped with a slice of lime and fresh mint.

Moonlit Kitchen Tip
Many organic broths are now packaged in pourable paper cartons, perfect for chilling in the fridge, and so convenient.

SERVES 4

GOLDEN HARVEST SOUP

*This soothing, soul-warming soup, glowing with the pumpkin-orange colors of the season,
is perfect for grounding during the late harvest moon.
Make it as spicy or mild as your taste buds prefer.*

2 tablespoons olive oil

1 medium-sized sweet onion, peeled, diced

1 teaspoon ground ginger

1 tablespoon good curry powder (mild or hot), or to taste

5 carrots, peeled, processed, or finely chopped

2 sweet potatoes, peeled, cubed

1 (15-ounce) can puréed pumpkin

5 cups organic chicken or vegetable broth

1 (14-ounce) can light coconut milk

1 tablespoon light brown sugar

Red pepper flakes

Sea salt and freshly ground pepper

Garnish
Sour cream or organic, plain yogurt

Freshly grated nutmeg

In a large soup pot heat the olive oil over medium heat and cook the onion for 2 to 3 minutes. Add the ginger and curry powder, and stir; continue to cook the onion until it is soft and translucent. Add the carrots and sweet potatoes, stir, and cook for 5 minutes. Add the puréed pumpkin and stir with a spoon, mixing well. Pour in the chicken broth and bring the soup to a high simmer. Cover, turn down the heat, and continue to gently simmer for 30 minutes. Using a potato masher, gently mash the cubes of sweet potato. Add the coconut milk, brown sugar, and red pepper flakes to taste. Season with sea salt and pepper. Heat for another 10 minutes.

Garnish this festive warming soup with a swirl of sour cream or plain yogurt, and some freshly grated nutmeg.

Serving Suggestion
Serve with a basket of warm corn muffins.

SERVES 4 TO 6

SOUTHWESTERN PUMPKIN AND CRAB SOUP

This unbeatable combination of pumpkin laced with crabmeat
makes a truly special soup for gatherings.

2 tablespoons olive oil

1 sweet onion, peeled, diced

3 tablespoons dark brown sugar

1 teaspoon ground cumin

½ teaspoon chili powder

1 (15-ounce) can puréed pumpkin
   or squash

3 cups organic chicken or vegetable
   broth

1 cup half-and-half or coconut milk

2 tablespoons fresh lime juice

½ pound lump crabmeat, picked
   over

Freshly grated nutmeg

Sea salt and freshly ground pepper

Garnish
Chopped fresh cilantro or mint
Fresh lime slices

In a heavy soup pot, heat the olive oil over medium heat and sauté the onion for 5 minutes, until softened. Add the brown sugar, cumin, and chili powder, and stir well, cooking for 1 minute. Add the pumpkin and stir briefly. Add the broth and mix well. Bring to a gentle simmer, cover, and cook for 15 minutes.

Add the half-and-half, then the lime juice, crabmeat, and nutmeg, gently cooking for 5 minutes. Do not boil. Season with sea salt and freshly ground pepper to taste.

Serve immediately in colorful bowls. Garnish each serving with fresh cilantro and a slice of lime.

Moonlit Kitchen Tip for Vegetarians
Omit the crab and serve the soup with thick slices of grilled cornbread.

SERVES 4

SANTA FE CHICKEN SOUP

A quick and savory chicken soup steeped in the sunny Southwestern flavors of chilies and corn, perfect for busy goddesses who want to warm up on a shivery fall evening.

2 tablespoons olive oil

1 Spanish onion, peeled, diced

5 garlic cloves, peeled, minced

1 celery stalk, trimmed and diced

1 serrano pepper or chili pepper, cored, seeded, chopped fine

1 teaspoon chili powder, or to taste

1 teaspoon ground cumin

¾ pound boneless chicken breasts, cut into bite-size strips

Sea salt and freshly ground pepper

1 cup sliced mushrooms

1 (28-ounce) can whole tomatoes (with juice)

1 (4-ounce) can green chilies, drained, chopped

6 cups organic chicken broth or vegetable broth

2 cups frozen sweet corn

Juice of 1 fresh lime

½ cup loosely packed fresh cilantro, chopped

Garnish
Sour cream

Cilantro

Begin by warming the olive oil in a large soup pot. Add the onion and sauté for 1 or 2 minutes. Add the garlic, celery, pepper, chili powder, and cumin; stir and cook until the onion is translucent. Add the chicken strips, season with a dash of sea salt and freshly ground pepper, and stir-fry until the chicken begins to turn white. Add the mushrooms and continue to stir for 3 to 4 minutes.

Add the tomatoes and green chilies, and break apart the tomatoes with a wooden spoon. Pour in the chicken broth. Add the sweet corn. Bring the soup to a high simmer, then turn down the heat and allow it to gently simmer for about 25 to 30 minutes. Just before serving, add the lime juice and the cilantro. Stir and taste the soup broth for seasoning adjustments.

Serve in festive bowls and garnish with a swirl of sour cream and a sprinkle of cilantro.

Serving Suggestion
Savory Cheddar Biscuits (page 120) or a basket of warmed, buttered tortillas make a perfect accompaniment.

Moonlit Kitchen Tip for Vegetarians
Omit the chicken and add some slices of cooked veggie sausages or slices of Mexican baked tofu during the final 10 minutes of cooking.

SERVES 4

CHICKPEA SOUP WITH LEMON

*This Moroccan-inspired soup is a creamy and satisfying dish
for any cold weather moon supper.*

1 (15-ounce) can chickpeas
(garbanzo beans)

4 cups light organic chicken or
vegetable broth

1 teaspoon sea salt

4 garlic cloves, peeled

1 teaspoon ground cumin

¼ cup natural peanut butter,
almond, or sesame butter

¼ cup fresh lemon juice

1 teaspoon red red pepper flakes, or
to taste

Freshly ground pepper

Garnish

Cayenne pepper

Chopped fresh mint or parsley

Lemon juice

Extra virgin olive oil

Drain the liquid from the chickpeas into a large saucepan and add the broth; cook on medium-high heat.

In a food processor or blender, purée the chickpeas with the sea salt, garlic, cumin, peanut butter, and lemon juice until smooth and creamy. When the broth has reached a high simmer, whisk in the chickpea purée and season with the red pepper flakes and fresh pepper. Blend well. Cover, lower the heat, and simmer for 30 minutes.

When you are ready to serve, ladle the soup into deep bowls and garnish with a pinch of cayenne pepper, chopped mint, a sprinkle of lemon juice, and a swirl of extra virgin olive oil on top.

Serving Suggestion

Toasted pita breads brushed with herbed olive oil make a perfect accompaniment.

Moonlit Kitchen Tip

For a change of pace, serve this soup with a swirl of yogurt topped with finely diced red onion and sprigs of fresh mint.

SERVES 4

THREE SISTERS STEW

Native American ancestors planted corn, beans, and squash together.
This compatible combination is known as the Three Sisters.
Here is a stew that celebrates the wisdom of interdependence.

2 tablespoons olive oil

1 medium onion, peeled, diced

4 garlic cloves, peeled, minced

1 teaspoon ground cumin

1 teaspoon chili powder

½ pound yellow squash, cut
into half-moons

½ pound zucchini, cut into half-
moons

1½ cups fresh corn (cut from about
3 ears) or frozen kernels, thawed

5 cups organic chicken or vegetable
broth

1 (16-ounce) can of kidney beans,
drained and rinsed

1 (4-ounce) can chopped green
chilies, or ½ cup sliced
jalapenos, drained

1 cup vine-ripened small cherry
tomatoes, halved

1 tablespoon fresh lime juice

Sea salt and freshly ground pepper

2 tablespoons chopped fresh
cilantro

Garnish
Sour cream

In a heavy-bottomed soup pot, heat the olive oil over medium-high heat and sauté the onion until it softens, about 5 minutes. Add the garlic, cumin, and chili powder, and cook briefly, about 1 minute. Lower the heat to medium. Stir for a minute. Add the yellow squash, zucchini, and corn, stirring to coat with spices; cook for 5 minutes, until the squash is tender. Add the broth, beans, and green chilies; stir well. Cover and lower the heat to a gentle simmer for about 10 minutes. Add the tomatoes, lime juice, and cilantro. Season with sea salt and pepper.

Cook through for 1 minute and serve in festive bowls. Garnish with a swirl of light sour cream, if desired.

Serving Suggestion
Paired with *Indian Fry Bread* (page 115) this stew makes a hearty meal.

Moonlit Kitchen Tip
For a delicious variation of this theme, in the fall season substitute cubed acorn, butternut, or even pumpkin for the summer squashes.

Serves 6

Gifts from the Hearth . . .
Breads and Muffins

What can be more magical than making bread? Mix together a bit of flour, salt, warm water, yeast, and sugar, and watch magic happen! Dough bubbles, stretches, takes form, and rises with a distinct character all its own. The beauty of dough is its receptivity to flavorings, spices, and herbs. It is affected by weather, the mood of the cook, and unseen forces. So mix your batter with a light heart and think good thoughts!

OLIVE AND ROSEMARY-RAISIN FOCACCIA

Hearty and satisfying, Italian focaccia is easy to make,
especially if you have a bread machine, standing mixer, or food processor to mix the dough.
Even goddesses love their power tools.

1½ teaspoons active dry yeast

1¼ cups warm water (heated to 100 degrees)

2 tablespoons granulated sugar

4 cups unbleached all-purpose flour

1½ teaspoons fine sea salt

2 tablespoons olive oil

1½ teaspoons dried thyme

½ cup (4 ounces) chopped black olives

⅓ cup raisins

2 tablespoons fresh rosemary leaves, minced

Coarse sea salt

Extra virgin olive oil

For bread machines: Follow the manufacturer's instructions for making dough (but do not bake), leaving out the chopped olives and raisins.

If mixing the dough by hand: Dissolve the yeast in the warm water, add granulated sugar, and allow it to activate, about 5 minutes. Begin adding the flour and salt, and beat with a wooden spoon or paddle mixer. Add the oil and the thyme. After about 5 minutes, when the dough is sticky and elastic, turn it out onto a floured surface and knead until soft, about 10 minutes. Cover with oiled plastic wrap and let it rise in a warm place until doubled in size, about 90 minutes.

When the dough is ready, turn it out onto a floured surface and add the olives and raisins, folding them in and gently kneading the dough briefly to mix. Roll out the dough to ½-inch thickness (a 12- to 14-inch circle), place it on a floured baking sheet or pizza pan, and cover with oiled plastic wrap. Place in a warm area and allow the dough to rise. If pressed for time, as little as 20 minutes will suffice. If not, allow the dough to double in size, which will take about 90 minutes. Preheat the oven to 375 degrees. Remove the plastic, sprinkle with rosemary and coarse sea salt, and drizzle with olive oil. Bake for 20 minutes, or until the bread is golden brown and sounds hollow when tapped. Cool briefly on a wire rack, and serve warm, with a communal dipping plate of extra virgin olive oil.

SERVES 6 TO 8

SAVORY MUFFINS

*A delightful combination of pecans and Parmesan makes these savory muffins
a perfect "bread" for soups, casseroles, and roasted dinners.
Add a dash of appropriate herbs to bake up some kitchen magic.*

1½ cups unbleached all-purpose flour

½ cup freshly grated Parmesan cheese

1 teaspoon baking powder

2 tablespoons light brown sugar

1 teaspoon fine sea salt

Pinch cayenne pepper or curry powder

1 teaspoon magical herb of choice, such as rosemary or thyme (optional)

2 large free-range eggs

½ cup light olive or vegetable oil

1 cup milk

⅔ cup chopped pecans

Preheat the oven to 375 degrees.

Lightly grease 12 muffin cups. In a large mixing bowl whisk together the flour, Parmesan cheese, baking powder, brown sugar, sea salt, cayenne pepper, and magical herb of your choice.

In a separate bowl beat the eggs and oil, add the milk, and blend well. Add the wet ingredients to the dry ingredients, stirring gently to combine. Stir in the chopped pecans. Divide the batter evenly among the muffin cups. Bake the muffins on the center oven rack for about 20 to 25 minutes, or until they are golden brown and a toothpick inserted into the center emerges clean. Cool the muffin pan on a rack for 5 minutes before removing the muffins.

Serve warm, with butter.

MAKES 12 MUFFINS

ORANGE-WALNUT SCONES

You'll love these traditional scones laced with the fresh taste of citrus, inviting happiness, fidelity, and affection. Visualize love and contentment as you stir the batter deosil (clockwise).

2 cups unbleached all-purpose flour

¼ cup light brown sugar

2 teaspoons baking soda

2 teaspoons baking powder

½ teaspoon salt

½ cup (1 stick) unsalted butter, chilled and cut into pieces, or ½ cup vegetable shortening

1 tablespoon freshly grated orange zest

½ cup milk or soy milk

1 large free-range egg, lightly beaten

½ cup organic, plain yogurt or sour cream

½ cup chopped walnuts or pecans

¼ cup turbinado (raw) sugar or light brown sugar

Preheat the oven to 400 degrees.

In a large mixing bowl combine the flour, brown sugar, baking soda, baking powder, and salt. Add the chilled butter, orange zest, milk, egg, and yogurt, and blend until ingredients are mixed, taking care not to overbeat the batter. Fold in the nuts. The batter for scones should be a bit dry, but if it's too dry, simply add a splash of milk to moisten it a little. Turn the dough out onto a lightly floured board, and knead for 1 minute.

Roll the dough out until about ¾ inch thick, and cut into wedges. Sprinkle the wedges with raw sugar, and place them on a baking sheet. Bake for about 15 to 20 minutes, until they are a light golden-brown color.

Serving Suggestion

Serve with butter and ginger jam for breakfast, or pair with *Roasted Vegetable Chowder* (page 95) for a light, satisfying supper.

MAKES 6 TO 8 SCONES

MAPLE-NUT MUFFINS

Old-fashioned flavors make this muffin both comforting and not-too-sweet.
Serve them to someone who needs a little maple magic.

2 cups unbleached all-purpose flour

1 teaspoon baking powder

1 teaspoon baking soda

¼ teaspoon fine sea salt

⅓ light brown sugar

¼ cup vegetable oil

½ cup real maple syrup

½ cup organic, plain yogurt or sour cream

1 large free-range egg

1 teaspoon pure vanilla extract

½ cup chopped pecans or walnuts (optional)

Preheat the oven to 350 degrees.

Lightly grease 8 muffin cups.

In a mixing bowl combine the flour, baking powder, baking soda, sea salt, and brown sugar. Set aside.

Beat the oil and maple syrup with an electric mixer for 2 minutes. Add the yogurt, egg, and vanilla. Slowly add the dry ingredients, mixing just until blended. Stir in the pecans. Pour the batter evenly into the greased muffin cups. Bake for 25 to 30 minutes, or until a toothpick inserted in the center emerges clean. Remove the muffins from the pan, and cool slightly on a wire rack.

Serve these delightful muffins while still warm.

MAKES 8 MUFFINS

LEMON BREAD

Bring the tart and juicy flavor of lemon to your Beltane table.
This bread is sublime on its own, fabulous for breakfast in bed, and splendid with a meal.

6 tablespoons unsalted butter or stick margarine, softened

1 cup light brown sugar, firmly packed

2 large free-range eggs, beaten

¼ cup sour cream or organic yogurt

1 tablespoon grated lemon zest

2 cups unbleached all-purpose flour

1½ teaspoons baking powder

1 teaspoon fine sea salt

⅓ cup chopped walnuts (optional)

Glaze

⅓ cup superfine granulated sugar

Juice of 1 lemon

Preheat the oven to 350 degrees.

Lightly grease an 8½-inch loaf pan.

Cream together the butter and brown sugar in a mixing bowl. Beat in the eggs and mix well. Add the sour cream and lemon zest, and beat until smooth.

In a separate bowl combine the flour, baking powder, and sea salt. Add the dry ingredients to the wet, and mix well. Fold in the chopped nuts, if desired. Spoon the batter into the greased loaf pan, and bake for about 50 minutes, or until a toothpick inserted into the center emerges clean.

Remove the bread from the oven, and make tiny holes in the top with a toothpick.

In a glass measuring cup whisk together the granulated sugar and lemon juice, until the sugar is dissolved. Slowly pour the lemon glaze on top of the loaf while it is still warm, allowing the glaze to seep into the bread. Set the loaf on a rack to cool for about 15 minutes. Turn it out of the pan and cool completely.

MAKES 1 LOAF

ORANGE TEA BREAD

A delightfully sunny quick bread that's perfect for an afternoon tea, or a sweet change of pace in the dinner bread basket. Oranges invite happiness and love!

2 cups unbleached all-purpose flour

1½ teaspoons baking powder

1 teaspoon fine sea salt

2 large free-range eggs

½ cup vegetable oil

½ cup sour cream or organic yogurt

1 tablespoon orange zest

¾ cup light brown sugar, packed

½ cup orange juice

⅓ cup currants

Glaze

1 tablespoon orange juice

1 tablespoon superfine granulated sugar

Preheat the oven to 350 degrees.

Grease an 8½-inch loaf pan.

In a mixing bowl combine the flour, baking powder, and sea salt.

In a separate bowl beat the eggs with the oil and sour cream until blended. Add the orange zest and brown sugar. Beat until smooth. Add the dry ingredients, alternating with the orange juice, and mix well. Fold in the currants. Pour into the greased loaf pan. Bake the loaf for 50 to 60 minutes, until a toothpick inserted in the center emerges clean.

Cool the bread on a rack for 10 minutes.

While the bread is cooling, make the glaze by whisking the orange juice with the granulated sugar.

Brush the glaze on the bread with a pastry brush. Return the loaf to the oven and bake for 1 minute to melt the glaze. Cool for 10 minutes before removing the bread from the pan, then allow the loaf to cool completely on a wire rack.

Moonlit Kitchen Tip

This recipe doubles well: make two loaves and pop one in the freezer.

SERVES 8

INDIAN FRY BREAD

*One of my all-time favorite breads, fry bread is a popular gift from Native American
cuisine. Here is my recipe, conjured up in Colorado,
after experimenting with several variations.*

1 package quick-rising yeast

2 tablespoons honey

1 teaspoon sea salt

2 teaspoons baking powder

4 cups unbleached all-purpose flour

1½ cups warm water

Canola or peanut oil for frying

Combine the yeast, honey, sea salt, baking powder, and flour with the warm water in a large mixing bowl, and knead the dough until it is soft. Cover with a damp towel (or oiled plastic wrap) and set aside for 30 minutes to let the dough rise. Remove the dough to a floured surface and divide it into 3-inch balls. Flatten the balls into circles about ¼ inch thick, and allow them to rest and rise for approximately 15 minutes.

Prepare for frying by pouring 1 to 2 inches of fresh canola oil into a deep heavy skillet and heating carefully over medium-high heat. To fry the dough, use tongs to place the dough into the oil, and fry one at a time for about 1½ minutes on each side, or until the dough is golden brown. Remove carefully from the hot oil. Set pieces on paper towels to drain. Gather them into a basket, and serve immediately, while they are still warm.

Moonlit Kitchen Tip

Some cooks first poke a tiny hole into the center of the dough to keep it from puffing out. Others would never think of doing such a thing! It's up to you. Enjoy *Indian Fry Bread* unadorned, or drizzle with honey to accompany very spicy foods and hot chilies. Sprinkled with cinnamon-sugar, they make a perfect breakfast treat. Smother them with your favorite chili or taco fillings and you have a hearty Indian taco!

MAKES ABOUT 6 BREADS

CHILI CORNBREAD

Native American flavors combine perfectly in this hearty, spicy classic.
Stir up some love and passion while you add red pepper flakes to the batter.

¼ cup light olive oil or corn oil

1¼ cups yellow cornmeal

¾ cup unbleached all-purpose flour

1 teaspoon baking soda

2 teaspoons baking powder

½ teaspoon sea salt

¼ cup granulated sugar

2 large free-range eggs, beaten

1 cup frozen corn kernels, drained
    well

¼ cup chopped green chilies,
    drained

1 cup milk or buttermilk

½ cup grated Monterey Jack or
    cheddar cheese

½ to 1 teaspoon red pepper flakes
    or chili powder, or to taste

Preheat the oven to 400 degrees.

Oil a 9 by 9-inch square baking pan.

Combine all of the ingredients in a mixing bowl and blend lightly, keeping the mixture a bit lumpy. Pour the batter into the prepared baking pan and sprinkle extra red pepper flakes or chili powder on the top.

Bake for 25 minutes, or until the center springs back when touched. Let the bread rest in the pan for 5 to 10 minutes before cutting.

SERVES 6

CINNAMON ZUCCHINI BREAD

Harvest moon means an abundance of zucchini and summer squashes.
Make several loaves of this cinnamon-laced bread to honor and enjoy your garden's abun-
dance, and welcome prosperity, love, and increased psychic awareness into your life.

3 cups unbleached all-purpose flour

1 teaspoon baking powder

1 teaspoon baking soda

1 teaspoon fine sea salt

1 tablespoon cinnamon

3 large free-range eggs, lightly
  beaten

1 cup canola or vegetable oil

2 cups light brown sugar, firmly
  packed

2 teaspoons pure vanilla extract

2 cups freshly grated zucchini,
  drained on paper towel

1 cup chopped walnuts or pecans
  (optional)

Preheat the oven to 325 degrees.

Oil and flour 2 8½-inch loaf pans.

In a mixing bowl combine the flour, baking powder, baking soda, sea salt, and cinnamon. Add the eggs, oil, brown sugar, and vanilla, and beat until blended. Fold in the zucchini and walnuts. Divide the batter between the loaf pans. Bake for 1 hour or until a toothpick inserted in the center emerges clean. Cool the pans on a rack before you turn out the loaves. Store the bread tightly wrapped in plastic wrap or aluminum foil.

Moonlit Kitchen Tip
Quick breads often taste even better the next day, so plan ahead and bake them now for eating later.

SERVES 8 PER LOAF

PUMPKIN MOON BREAD

*Honor all the autumn moons with this richly delicious bread infused with grounding
aromatic spices. Why witches love pumpkin recipes is probably no mystery.
This magical recipe invites love and cultivates both inner fire and spiritual protection.*

2 cups unbleached all-purpose flour

1½ teaspoons baking powder

1 teaspoon baking soda

1 teaspoon fine sea salt

2 teaspoons cinnamon

1 teaspoon pumpkin pie spice

1½ cups light brown sugar

2 large free-range eggs, beaten

⅔ cup canola oil or vegetable oil

¼ cup orange juice

1 cup pumpkin purée (canned is
   fine)

1 teaspoon pure vanilla extract

Preheat the oven to 350 degrees.

Grease a 9-inch loaf pan.

Sift together the flour, baking powder, baking soda, sea salt, cinnamon, and pumpkin pie spice.

In a separate mixing bowl combine the brown sugar, eggs, oil, orange juice, pumpkin, and vanilla; beat until blended. Add the dry ingredients, and beat until the batter is smooth. Pour the batter into the greased loaf pan, and bake for 50 minutes or until a toothpick inserted into the center emerges clean. Allow the loaf to cool in the pan for 10 minutes before carefully turning it out onto a rack to cool completely.

Moonlit Kitchen Tip

Lining the bottom of the loaf pan with buttered parchment paper makes it easier to ease the loaf from the pan.

MAKES 1 9-INCH LOAF

CAPE COD BANNOCK

*One of the earliest known "quick breads," bannocks were originally a simple blend of flour,
salt, and a bit of bacon fat cooked over an open fire. My own version adds a little sweetness,
accented with Cape Cod's native cranberries.*

3 cups unbleached all-purpose flour

⅓ cup light brown sugar, packed

2 teaspoons baking powder

1 teaspoon baking soda

1 teaspoon fine sea salt

½ cup sour cream

1½ cups buttermilk

½ cup sweetened dried cranberries

Preheat the oven to 350 degrees.

Lightly oil and flour an 8- or 9-inch cake pan or a heavy baking sheet.

Stir together the flour, brown sugar, baking powder, baking soda, and sea salt in a mixing bowl. Gently add the sour cream and buttermilk until the dough is soft, taking care not to overblend. Fold in the cranberries. Turn the dough out onto a generously floured surface, and briefly knead with floured hands until the dough forms a smooth ball. Pat the dough into a circle about 1 inch thick. Place in the lightly oiled and floured cake pan. Using a sharp floured knife, cut a cross approximately ½ inch deep into the top of the dough (this is to keep the fairies at bay).

Bake the bannock for 30 to 35 minutes, until it is golden brown. Set it on a rack to cool for at least 15 minutes before cutting and serving.

Serving Suggestion

Serve warm bannock with plenty of butter and jam for breakfast or afternoon tea. For a light supper, serve warm bannock with a bowl of soup.

SERVES 8

SAVORY CHEDDAR BISCUITS

These biscuits are a family favorite. Quick to toss together, they taste best warm from the oven. Add a pinch or two of the appropriate spice to enhance any magical intention.

2 cups all-purpose flour

1½ teaspoons baking powder

1 teaspoon baking soda

1 teaspoon salt

1 tablespoon granulated sugar

½ cup vegetable shortening or butter

⅔ cup shredded cheddar cheese

¾ cup milk

1 tablespoon sherry (optional)

¼ teaspoon cayenne pepper, or to taste

Preheat the oven to 400 degrees.

In a large mixing bowl combine the flour, baking powder, baking soda, salt, and granulated sugar. Cut in the shortening, using a pastry blender or 2 knives, until it resembles coarse meal. Add the shredded cheese, milk, sherry, and cayenne pepper, and stir just until the dry ingredients are moist. Do not overblend. Turn the dough out onto a lightly floured surface, and knead lightly about 5 times. Less handling keeps the dough tender.

Roll out the dough to about ½ inch thick, and cut 2-inch rounds using a floured juice glass or cookie cutter. Place the biscuits on an ungreased baking sheet, and bake for 10 to 12 minutes, until they are golden brown.

Moonlit Kitchen Tip
For a Southwestern twist add ¼ cup drained, chopped green chilies.

MAKES ABOUT 15 BISCUITS

BLUEBERRY BREAD

You don't have to wait until a blue moon to enjoy this yummy bread.
Use freshly picked blueberries in the summer, or frozen blueberries during the colder months.

2½ cups unbleached all-purpose flour

3 teaspoons baking powder

½ teaspoon fine sea salt

1 cup granulated sugar

⅔ cup light brown sugar, firmly packed

¼ teaspoon ground nutmeg

2 large free-range eggs, beaten

½ cup vegetable oil or melted butter

1½ teaspoons pure vanilla extract

½ cup milk

1 cup blueberries, washed, tossed in a little flour

Preheat the oven to 350 degrees.

Grease a 9-inch loaf pan.

Sift together the flour, baking powder, and sea salt. Add the granulated sugar, brown sugar, and nutmeg. Lightly combine the eggs, oil, vanilla, and milk in a large bowl. Pour the wet mixture into the dry mixture and blend lightly. Gently fold in the blueberries. Pour the batter into the greased loaf pan.

Bake for 50 to 60 minutes, until a toothpick inserted into the center emerges clean. Cool the loaf on a rack for 10 or 15 minutes. Carefully loosen the loaf around the edges with a plastic spatula, and remove from the pan.

SERVES 4 TO 6

Main Dishes

The time to celebrate is now. The Goddess' bounty is here today. Fabulous fowl, gifts from the sea, grains, and divine pastas delight our palate and satisfy our hunger. Stir your best intentions with your seasonings. Cook consciously, and create love, harmony, and healing magic in your kitchen. Culinary magic is an ancient art form that nourishes the body and feeds the soul. Vegetarian versions are given at the end of each recipe.

LEMON VEGETABLE PENNE WITH PINE NUTS

This light lemony pasta is a treat for the senses. Serve it with a crisp Chardonnay wine in chilled glasses, and toast Hera as the Goddess of Midsummer.

1 pound Italian penne pasta

⅛ cup extra virgin olive oil

3 tablespoons olive oil

4 garlic cloves, peeled, minced

1 tablespoon fresh lemon zest

2 teaspoons red pepper flakes, or to taste

1 sweet red pepper, seeded, chopped

2 cups broccoli florets, bite-size pieces

2 Portobello mushrooms, sliced

½ cup pine nuts

⅔ cup white wine

Juice of 1 lemon

½ cup fresh Italian parsley, chopped

¾ cup freshly grated Parmesan cheese

Sea salt and freshly ground pepper

Garnish
Fresh Italian parsley, chopped
Freshly grated Parmesan cheese

Bring a large pot of salted water to a rolling boil and cook the penne according to package directions until it is al dente. Drain and reserve some of the cooking liquid. Toss the pasta in ⅛ cup extra virgin olive oil and set aside.

While the pasta is cooking, heat the 3 tablespoons olive oil in a large pan over medium heat and gently sauté the garlic for 1 minute. Add the lemon zest and red pepper flakes, and stir for 2 minutes. (Do not brown the garlic.) Add the red pepper, broccoli florets, Portobello mushrooms, and pine nuts, and cook until the vegetables are tender, stirring occasionally, for about 7 minutes. Add the wine, lemon juice, and cooked pasta. Sprinkle the parsley and Parmesan on top, and toss well. Season with sea salt and freshly ground pepper to taste. (If the pasta seems a little dry, add some of the reserved pasta cooking liquid.)

Serve at once in warmed pasta bowls topped with a flourish of fresh chopped parsley. Offer extra grated Parmesan at the table.

SERVES 4

SAVORY GLAZED TURKEY "MEAT LOAF"

A leaner alternative to an old-fashioned favorite.
Generous seasoning makes the difference between boring and fantastic!

2 pounds ground turkey, organic if
   available

1 sweet onion, peeled, diced

3 garlic cloves, peeled, minced

¾ cup jarred roasted red peppers,
   drained and chopped

1 cup chopped mushrooms, or
   diced celery and carrots

2 large free-range eggs, slightly
   beaten

3 tablespoons Worcestershire sauce

1 cup coarse bread crumbs

½ cup catsup

½ teaspoon ground cumin

½ teaspoon ground nutmeg

Dash of curry powder, or
   cinnamon, sea salt, and
   pepper

Preheat the oven to 350 degrees.

In a large mixing bowl combine the ground turkey, onion, garlic, peppers, mushrooms, eggs, Worcestershire sauce, bread crumbs, catsup, cumin, nutmeg, and curry powder. Gently mix with a fork until all the ingredients are mixed well and evenly distributed. Spoon the turkey mixture into 9-inch nonstick loaf pan, pressing down to compact the loaf. Smooth out the top, making sure that the top of the loaf is ½ inch below the rim of the pan (this is so there is enough room in the pan to contain the glaze drippings). Bake the turkey loaf for 30 minutes.

Mix the glaze ingredients in a glass measuring cup, stirring until the brown sugar is dissolved. Open the oven door, partially pull out the oven rack, and carefully pour the glaze over the top of the loaf. If you have extra glaze, use a fork to pierce the loaf top, pour the rest of the glaze on top, and let the glaze soak in a bit. Return the loaf to the oven and bake for another 30 minutes.

Let the turkey loaf rest in the pan for 5 minutes before slicing. This will help it to settle, and keep it from falling apart.

Glaze

⅓ cup catsup

⅓ cup honey or maple syrup

⅓ cup light brown sugar

½ teaspoon prepared mustard
(preferably honey or spicy)

Dash of nutmeg

Serving Suggestion

If you are lucky enough to have leftovers, this turkey loaf is delicious the next day, served cold on thick slices of rustic bread smeared with a savory mustard.

Moonlit Kitchen Tip for Vegetarians

Craving meatloaf? Use soy protein instead of ground turkey. Crumble up 2 pounds of veggie burgers, and moisten with soy milk as needed (approximately ½ cup), and add the rest of the ingredients. Proceed with the recipe.

SERVES 4 TO 6

BAKED CHICKEN BREASTS
IN LEMON TARRAGON CREAM

*Be the reigning goddess in your kitchen by serving this romantic dish
smothered in a lemon and tarragon cream.*

4 boneless, skinless, free-range
chicken breast halves (about 5
ounces each)

½ cup unbleached all-purpose flour
for dredging

Sea salt and freshly ground pepper

2 tablespoons olive oil

2 garlic cloves, peeled, minced

½ cup dry white wine or dry
vermouth

2 to 3 teaspoons freshly grated
lemon zest

Preheat the oven to 375 degrees.

Rinse the chicken breasts well and pat dry. In a shallow bowl or dish, season the flour with sea salt and pepper, and dredge the chicken breasts, coating both sides; set aside.

In a medium skillet heat the olive oil over medium-high heat, and add the garlic, stirring for just a moment. Carefully add the dredged chicken and lightly sear the pieces on both sides until they are golden brown, about 3 minutes per side.

Scrape down the browned bits in the skillet with a wooden spoon and add the wine, stirring for 1 or 2 minutes, as you deglaze the pan. Remove from the heat. Make the *Lemon Tarragon Cream.*

Lemon Tarragon Cream

1 cup light or regular sour cream,
   thinned with ¼ cup half-and-half
   or light cream
1 tablespoon freshly squeezed
   lemon juice
1 teaspoon dried tarragon
Dash of half-and-half

Lemon Tarragon Cream

Combine the sour cream, lemon juice, and tarragon in a mixing cup and whisk till smooth. Add a dash of half-and-half to thin it a bit.

Pour the tarragon cream into the skillet, whisking to blend the cream sauce with the wine reduction and tasty bits.

Place the chicken breasts in a lightly oiled baking dish, and pour the *Lemon Tarragon Cream* over the pieces. Sprinkle with the grated lemon zest.

Bake for 20 to 30 minutes, until the center of the thickest chicken breast no longer looks pink, but remains juicy.

Serving Suggestion

Serve at once on a bed of *Creamy Garlic Grits* (page 149) or a generous spoonful of steamed basmati rice.

Moonlit Kitchen Tip for Vegetarians

Substitute 3 to 4 large Portobello mushroom caps, sliced thickly, for the chicken. Forgo the dredging with flour, and sauté directly. Proceed with the recipe.

SERVES 4

BALSAMIC ROASTED CHICKEN WITH PEPPERS

*The heady fragrance that fills the house while these potent flavors roast and mingle
draws kin and guests into the kitchen, mouths watering and expectant.
Offer them a plate of olives and a glass of wine to comfort their taste buds while they wait.*

4 boneless, skinless, free-range
   chicken breast halves

Sea salt and freshly ground pepper

2 tablespoons olive oil

6 tablespoons extra virgin olive oil

1 large sweet onion, peeled,
   chopped

1½ large red peppers, seeded, cut
   into thin strips

1 large green bell pepper, seeded,
   cut into thin strips

1 garlic clove, peeled, minced

½ cup balsamic vinegar

1 tablespoon fresh marjoram
   leaves, or 1 to 2 teaspoons dried

Preheat the oven to 400 degrees.

Pour a little oil into the bottom of a roasting pan, and spread it around a bit with your fingers.

Rinse the chicken breasts under cold water, pat them dry, and place them in the roasting pan. Wash your hands. Season the chicken with a little sea salt and pepper.

Heat 2 tablespoons of olive oil in a skillet and sauté the onion for 5 minutes. Add the peppers and stir until they are soft, about 5 to 7 minutes. Remove from the heat. Spoon the onion and peppers over the chicken breasts. Sprinkle the garlic all over the chicken. Now combine the 6 tablespoons of extra virgin olive oil and balsamic vinegar with the marjoram in a glass measuring cup, stir, and pour evenly over the seasoned onion, peppers, and chicken.

Roast in the oven for about 20 to 25 minutes, checking halfway through, and spooning some of the balsamic sauce from the sides of the pan over the top of the chicken breasts. The chicken is cooked when it is no longer pink in the center; it should be white, but still juicy.

Place each chicken breast on a warmed plate. Spoon any remaining sauce over the top of each serving, and dust with a spoonful of Parmesan cheese. Sprinkle a tablespoon of parsley over each plate with a flourish!

Garnish

Freshly grated Parmesan cheese

4 tablespoons fresh parsley, chopped

Serving Suggestion

Serve with a large spoonful of *Karri Ann's Colcannon* (page 152), or hot buttered linguini pasta smothered with balsamic roasted onions and peppers. Include a warm crusty loaf of peasant-style bread and a dipping plate of extra virgin olive oil, and serve with goblets of robust red table wine.

Moonlit Kitchen Tip for Vegetarians

Instead of chicken, use Portobello mushroom caps, sliced thickly, or veggie sausages.

SERVES 4

GRECIAN QUICHE

Aphrodite herself might have whipped up this simple yet romantic dish.
It's also perfect for brunch or breakfast in bed . . .

1 tablespoon olive oil

½ sweet onion, peeled, chopped

¾ cup roasted red peppers, drained, chopped

Pinch of Greek oregano or marjoram

4 large free-range eggs or egg substitute

½ cup milk

¾ cup half-and-half

Sea salt and freshly ground pepper

1 prepared frozen 8- or 9-inch piecrust (Aphrodite devotes her time to the pursuit of love and beauty, not piecrusts from scratch, you know . . .)

4 ounces chèvre or cheddar cheese

⅓ cup black (ripe) olives, lightly chopped

Preheat the oven to 400 degrees.

In a medium skillet heat the olive oil on medium heat and add the sweet onion, sautéing until the onion begins to soften, about 4 or 5 minutes. Remove from the heat, add the roasted peppers and oregano, and stir. Set the pan aside.

In a large glass measuring cup whisk the eggs lightly, add the milk and half-and-half, and whisk again. Stir in a dash of sea salt and freshly ground pepper. Ready your prepared crust. Cut or break apart the chèvre into small pieces as best you can, and scatter half of the cheese over the bottom of the piecrust. Spoon the sautéed onion and pepper mixture into the crust, and distribute the rest of the cheese on top. Add the chopped black olives. Pour the egg mixture gently into the crust. It should be just shy of the inner top edge. (Be careful not to overfill.)

Carefully place the quiche into the middle of the hot oven, and bake for 30 to 35 minutes, until the filling is set, puffy, and *lightly* browned. Allow the quiche to cool and settle for 10 minutes before cutting and serving.

Serving Suggestion

When serving for brunch or a light supper, accompany the pie with a crisp green salad, soft fresh pita breads with butter, and chilled white wine. If serving *Grecian Quiche* in bed, I recommend using a tray. . . . Gather some assorted fresh fruit, and fill stemmed glasses with orange juice and a splash of champagne. Leftovers are wonderful cold.

Moonlit Kitchen Tip

Place your prepared piecrust on a round pizza pan or sturdy cooking sheet before you begin filling it. This helps to stabilize the filled crust as you place it into the oven.

SERVES 4 AS A MAIN COURSE,
OR 6 AS A SIDE DISH

ATHENA'S OLIVE AND ARTICHOKE CHICKEN ON ANGEL HAIR PASTA

A divine pasta inspired by the Goddess Athena, whose gift to early Greeks was the olive tree.

2 tablespoons olive oil

4 garlic cloves, peeled, minced

4 boneless, skinless, free-range chicken breasts, cut into strips

2 (6.5-ounce) jars marinated quartered artichoke hearts, drained

2 tablespoons capers, rinsed and drained

⅔ cup coarsely chopped black (ripe) olives

½ cup dry white wine

Juice of 1 fresh lemon

½ cup organic chicken or vegetable broth

1 teaspoon dried oregano

1 tablespoon chopped fresh mint

Sea salt and freshly ground pepper

1 pound angel hair pasta

6 tablespoons extra virgin olive oil

Garnish

¾ cup crumbled feta cheese

Heat a large pot of salted water (for the pasta). Note that it only takes about 2 minutes to cook angel hair pasta, so it should be prepared at the end, just before the chicken is ready.

Heat 2 tablespoons olive oil in a large skillet on medium heat, and quickly sauté the garlic for 1 minute. Add the chicken strips and sauté for 3 minutes, until they are lightly browned. Add the artichokes, capers, olives, wine, and half of the lemon juice, and cook for 1 or 2 minutes, until the wine reduces a bit. Add the broth and herbs, and season with sea salt and freshly ground pepper to taste. Cover and lower the heat to medium-low, and cook for another 3 minutes. (The chicken is done when it is no longer pink inside.)

Meanwhile, cook the angel hair pasta (but be careful not to overcook!). It's best if served al dente, with some texture. When the pasta is ready, drain, then pour it into a warmed serving bowl. Toss it with 6 tablespoons extra virgin olive oil and the rest of the lemon juice. Add the chicken mixture from the skillet and lightly toss. Sprinkle the feta cheese over the pasta for garnish, and serve country style, at the table.

Serving Suggestion

Offer a basket brimming with fresh crusty bread, extra virgin olive oil for dipping, and goblets of crisp white wine.

Moonlit Kitchen Tip for Vegetarians

Instead of chicken, use 1 bunch of fresh spinach, washed and stemmed, and 2 large Portobello mushroom caps, sliced. Use soy cheese. Slices of savory baked tofu also make a tasty substitute.

SERVES 4

CRABMEAT ENCHILADAS

One of the Goddess' gifts from the sea, sweet crab meat makes a light and delectable filling for corn tortillas baked in a green chili tomato sauce, topped with melting Monterey Jack cheese.

Filling

1 pound snow or imitation crabmeat, flaked

4 green onions, peeled, chopped (white section only)

2 to 3 garlic cloves, peeled, minced

Juice of ½ lemon

1 teaspoon Dijon mustard

1 teaspoon Old Bay Seasoning

Freshly ground pepper

3 tablespoons sour cream

10 fresh corn tortillas

3 to 4 cups *Green Chili Tomato Sauce*

1 cup grated Monterey Jack or soy cheese

Garnish

Sour cream

Freshly chopped cilantro

Preheat the oven to 350 degrees.

Combine the crabmeat with the green onions, garlic, lemon juice, mustard, Old Bay Seasoning, and pepper in a bowl; toss to mix. Add the sour cream, stirring to blend well.

Lightly oil a baking pan that will fit 10 enchiladas snugly. Divide the crabmeat filling among the 10 tortillas, then spoon the portions into the center of each tortilla, roll, and place seam side down in the baking dish. Pour the *Green Chili Tomato Sauce* over the assembled enchiladas, and top with the grated Monterey Jack cheese. Bake uncovered for about 25 minutes, until the enchiladas are bubbling and the cheese is melted.

Garnish with a spoonful of sour cream and a sprinkling of freshly chopped cilantro.

Green Chili Tomato Sauce

1 to 2 tablespoons olive oil

1 small onion, peeled, finely chopped

½ teaspoon chili powder

½ teaspoon ground cumin

1 garlic clove, peeled, minced

2 cups crushed tomatoes or 1 (16-ounce) can crushed tomatoes

1 (14-ounce) can green chilies, drained well, chopped

Dash of sherry or red wine vinegar

Green Chili Tomato Sauce

Heat the olive oil in a medium saucepan, and sauté the onion, chili powder, and cumin for 5 minutes. Add the garlic and cook for another 3 minutes. Add the tomatoes and green chilies, and add a dash of sherry. Bring the sauce to a medium simmer, cover, and lower the heat, allowing it to simmer for 15 minutes.

Serving Suggestion

Serve the enchiladas with seasoned rice and a mixed summer squash and onion sauté. Cool and refrigerate any leftover *Green Chili Tomato Sauce* in a covered non-metallic container and use for any Southwestern-style dish.

Moonlit Kitchen Tip for Vegetarians

Instead of crabmeat, use cooked pinto beans.

SERVES 4

BARBECUED FISH IN FOIL PACKETS

Try this simple savory recipe for fish on one of those long hot July days. Why heat up the kitchen when you can fire up the grill and sip lemonade in the hammock instead? We summer goddesses know how to keep our cool.

4 serving-size pieces of scrod, haddock, or cod, rinsed and patted dry

Juice of 1 lime

Sea salt and freshly ground pepper

1 red onion, peeled, thinly sliced

8 garlic cloves, peeled, minced

1 green bell pepper, cored, seeded, thinly sliced

1 yellow pepper, cored, seeded, thinly sliced

4 tablespoons extra virgin olive oil plus additional olive oil for oiling the aluminum foil

4 tablespoons balsamic vinegar

½ cup of your favorite spicy barbecue/grilling sauce

½ cup chopped fresh parsley or cilantro

4 bay leaves

Garnish
Lime wedges

Preheat grill to medium-high heat.

Lay out 4 10-inch squares of aluminum foil, and lightly oil the center of each square with a little olive oil. Place 1 piece of fish in the center of each. Squeeze lime juice over each piece and season with sea salt and freshly ground pepper. Scatter the onion, garlic, and peppers over each piece of fish.

In a glass measuring cup mix together the 4 tablespoons olive oil, balsamic vinegar, and barbecue sauce. Drizzle the sauce over each serving of fish, and top with a spoonful of fresh parsley or cilantro. Add 1 bay leaf per packet. Fold the foil up and crimp the edges together to create sealed packages.

Cook the fish on the hot grill, covered, for 7 to 15 minutes, depending upon the thickness and size of the fish. The fish is done when it is opaque and flakes easily. Resist overcooking it.

Garnish with lime wedges.

Moonlit Kitchen Tip for Vegetarians

This recipe works well with veggie sausages. Use 2 onions instead of 1, and keep an eye on the timing, as the sausages should be cooked through and the veggies should be tender.

SERVES 4

BAKED RICOTTA CHICKEN ZITI

Here is everyone's favorite comfort food—with an Italian flair.
A perfect way to take advantage of leftover chicken.
Goddesses know how to utilize leftovers.

1 pound Italian ziti pasta

⅛ cup extra virgin olive oil

1½ to 2 cups cooked chicken, torn
   into bite-size pieces

½ cup sliced or slivered almonds

Sea salt and freshly ground pepper

2 tablespoons olive oil

1 onion, peeled, diced

3 garlic cloves, peeled, minced

1 (7-ounce) package fresh baby
   spinach leaves, rinsed, stemmed

¼ teaspoon nutmeg

2 teaspoons Worcestershire sauce

1 pound Italian ricotta cheese

½ cup freshly grated Parmesan or
   Romano cheese

Topping

¼ cup freshly grated Parmesan
   cheese

¼ cup sliced or slivered almonds, or
   whole pine nuts

½ cup Italian-style seasoned bread
   crumbs

2 tablespoons extra virgin olive oil

Preheat the oven to 375 degrees.

Bring a large pot of salted water to a rolling boil and cook the ziti for 9 to 10 minutes, until it is not quite al dente. (The ziti will continue to cook in the casserole later, so undercook it now.) Drain the pasta well, and pour into a large mixing bowl. Drizzle with ⅛ cup extra virgin olive oil and toss to coat well. Add the chicken and sliced almonds. Season with sea salt and pepper. Stir briefly.

In a medium-sized skillet, heat 2 tablespoons olive oil on medium heat, and gently cook the onion and garlic for about 7 minutes, until the onion is softened and translucent. Remove from the heat. Add the spinach leaves, and season with nutmeg and Worcestershire sauce. Stir well.

Add this skillet mixture to the pasta, along with the ricotta and Parmesan, and lightly toss the ingredients to mix well. Spoon the pasta mixture into an oiled 2-quart ovenproof casserole dish. Combine the topping ingredients in a small bowl and crumble over the top of the pasta. Bake for about 25 minutes, until the casserole bubbles and the topping is browned. Allow it to settle for 5 minutes before serving.

Moonlit Kitchen Tip for Vegetarians

Instead of chicken, use 2 large Portobello mushroom caps, cut into bite-size pieces, and sautée in a little olive oil until lightly browned. Proceed with the recipe.

Serves 6

PORTOBELLO AND CHICKEN STROGANOFF ON PARSLEY-BUTTERED NOODLES

My mother's stroganoff was the only meat dish I would eat as a child.
Recently, I began to crave it, and conjured up this recipe using chicken in place of beef.

2 to 3 tablespoons olive oil

1 onion, peeled, finely chopped

3 garlic cloves, peeled, minced

1 pound small to medium Portobello mushrooms, sliced into bite-size pieces

1 pound free-range boneless chicken breasts, cut into strips

2 tablespoons Worcestershire sauce

1 cup organic chicken or vegetable broth

1 tablespoon Dijon mustard

⅓ cup half-and-half or light cream

¾ cup sour cream

4 tablespoons dry sherry

1 to 2 tablespoons unbleached all-purpose flour

Sea salt and freshly ground pepper

2 tablespoons minced fresh dill

2 tablespoons chopped fresh parsley

8 ounces egg noodles, cooked, buttered, and tossed with 1 tablespoon fresh chopped parsley

Heat the olive oil in large nonstick skillet over medium heat, then sauté the onion, stirring for about 4 or 5 minutes, until the onion is softened. Add the garlic and mushrooms, and stir, cooking until the mushrooms are tender and starting to brown, about 10 minutes. Add the chicken strips and Worcestershire sauce, and stir, cooking the chicken for about 5 minutes. Remove the chicken and keep it warm.

Meanwhile, combine the broth, mustard, half-and-half, and sour cream in a large measuring cup. Lower the heat under the skillet, add the sherry, and deglaze the pan by scraping all the tasty bits of onion and garlic with a wooden spoon. Add the flour and stir for about 1 minute. Add the sour cream mixture, whisk, and bring to a gentle simmer, still whisking, until the sauce thickens, about 3 minutes. Return the chicken to the pan. Cover and lower the heat, simmering until the chicken is cooked through, about 5 minutes. (The chicken is done when it is no longer pink inside.) Taste the sauce for seasoning adjustments, and add sea salt and freshly ground pepper to taste. Add the dill and parsley, stir, and serve immediately over hot cooked parsleyed noodles or other pasta.

Moonlit Kitchen Tip for Vegetarians
Double the Portobello mushrooms and omit the chicken, and you have a lovely vegetarian stroganoff!

SERVES 4

ORANGE MARINATED SALMON

The sunny, fresh flavor of oranges permeates this impeccable celebratory dish.
Salmon signifies abundance, and oranges bring happiness and represent the sun,
making this a perfect choice for Yuletide gatherings.

4 salmon fillets (one per person)

1 orange, washed

¾ cup fresh orange juice

1 tablespoon fresh lemon juice

1 tablespoon sesame oil

1 tablespoon light brown sugar

1 tablespoon soy or Worcestershire
    sauce

1 teaspoon cornstarch

Sea salt and freshly ground pepper

Garnish
Fresh cilantro or parsley, chopped

Rinse the salmon fillets and pat dry.

Using a zester or grater, grate the orange until you have 1 tablespoon of orange zest. Remove the rest of the peel from the orange and pull out the sections, cleaning away the pith and seeds, and set the sections aside. Combine the orange zest, orange juice, lemon juice, sesame oil, brown sugar, soy sauce, and cornstarch in a bowl to make the marinade. Pour half of the marinade into a shallow glass dish. Place each of the salmon fillets into the dish, turning once to coat each piece with the marinade. Season with sea salt and freshly ground pepper.

Cover and refrigerate for 1 hour. Pour the remaining orange marinade into a small saucepan and bring to a simmer, stirring for 3 to 5 minutes, until it begins to reduce and thicken. Remove from the heat and add the cleaned orange sections.

Set your oven to broil.

Remove the salmon fillets from the marinade and place on a lightly oiled broiler pan, then *discard the marinade.* Broil the salmon 6 inches from the heat source for about 6 minutes. Remove from the oven.

To serve the salmon, plate each piece and spoon the reduced orange sauce and orange sections over the fillets. Sprinkle cilantro or parsley around the plate for garnish.

SERVES 4

ROASTED ONIONS, PORTOBELLO, AND GOAT CHEESE ON PUMPKIN POLENTA

*Following my own witchy intuition one autumn day, I roasted onions and Portobello mushrooms and paired them with **Pumpkin Polenta**. Here is the earthy and satisfying result.*

4 medium-large onions, peeled, cut into thick wedges

4 large Portobello mushroom caps, cleaned and sliced

6 garlic cloves, peeled, minced

¼ cup extra virgin olive oil

¼ cup balsamic vinegar

1 teaspoon dried marjoram or Italian herbs

Sea salt and freshly ground pepper

Preheat the oven to 400 degrees.

Combine the onions and Portobello mushroom caps in a roasting pan and sprinkle with the garlic.

In a glass measuring cup whisk the olive oil, balsamic vinegar, and marjoram. Pour the vinaigrette all over the vegetables and toss gently to coat. Season with sea salt and freshly ground pepper. Place the pan in the oven on the center rack and roast the vegetables until they are tender, about 30 to 40 minutes.

In the meantime, make the *Pumpkin Polenta*.

Pumpkin Polenta

5½ cups organic chicken or light
  vegetable broth

1½ cups polenta (stone-ground
  cornmeal)

¾ cup cooked (or canned)
  pumpkin

Sea salt and freshly ground pepper

4 ounces chèvre, cream cheese, or
  soy cream cheese

Pinch of freshly grated nutmeg

Garnish

Chèvre

Freshly grated nutmeg

Pumpkin Polenta

In a heavy-bottomed soup pot, bring the broth to a gentle boil. Begin slowly pouring the polenta into the pot as you stir with a whisk or wooden spoon. Turn down the heat to low. Continue to stir to keep the polenta smooth. After about 5 minutes, add the pumpkin and continue to stir. Season with sea salt and freshly ground pepper. Cook the polenta mixture, stirring well, until it is tender and has a creamy consistency, about 20 minutes. It will thicken and pull away from the sides of the pot when it is done. Stir the chèvre and some freshly grated nutmeg into the polenta just before serving.

Serve immediately. Spoon soft mounds onto each plate and top with the roasted onion and Portobello mixture.

Garnish each serving with crumbled chèvre and some freshly grated nutmeg.

Moonlit Kitchen Tip

Polenta can now be purchased in a quick-cooking style, cutting down the stirring time by more than half. Look for it in your local health-food store.

SERVES 4

SALMON-SCALLION CAKES
WITH LIME-HORSERADISH MAYONNAISE

This a goddess' answer to the mundane burger.
Savory salmon fries up golden and crispy on the outside, tender on the inside.

1 large free-range egg, beaten

1 pound cooked salmon (canned is fine), boned and flaked

1 teaspoon Dijon mustard

4 scallions, chopped (white and light-green parts only)

1 cup herbed or seasoned bread crumbs

½ teaspoon Old Bay Seasoning or curry powder

½ teaspoon dill

Dash of cayenne pepper

1 tablespoon fresh lime juice

2 tablespoons soft cream cheese or mayonnaise

Unbleached all-purpose flour for dredging

Olive oil for frying

Lime-Horseradish Mayonnaise

1 cup mayonnaise

1 tablespoon fresh lime juice

1 to 2 teaspoons horseradish, or to taste

1 teaspoon dried dill, or 1 tablespoon fresh mint, chopped

Combine the egg with the salmon in a bowl and gently add the mustard, scallions, bread crumbs, Old Bay Seasoning, dill, cayenne pepper, lime juice, and soft cream cheese until lightly blended. Form the mixture into 8 to 10 cakes and lightly dip each one into a plate dusted with flour. Set aside on a piece of wax paper.

Heat the olive oil in a skillet over medium heat and begin frying the cakes, setting them in the pan about 1 inch apart. Cook for about 3 minutes on the first side, until the bottom is golden. Turn the cakes over and fry them for another 2 minutes or so, until they are nicely browned and cooked through. Drain on paper towels, then serve with a dollop of *Lime-Horseradish Mayonnaise.*

Lime-Horseradish Mayonnaise

Combine all the ingredients in a small bowl and mix until smooth and creamy. Cover and chill until serving.

Serving Suggestion

Place cakes and a dollop of *Lime-Horseradish Mayonnaise* on a bed of fresh mesclun greens. The mayonnaise also makes a wonderful spread for sandwiches, grilled seafood, or roasted Portobello mushroom caps.

MAKES 8 TO 10 CAKES, AND 1 CUP OF MAYONNAISE

Side Dishes and Vegetables

Through the turning Wheel of the Year, our local markets inspire us with fresh seasonal produce, displayed in gorgeous bunches and baskets. Colors, textures, and unmistakable scents reflect the gifts of each season. The first asparagus of spring, summer's ripened tomatoes, or the pumpkins of fall help us to mark our year's journey through the thirteen moons. Create a magical and bountiful feast with several side dishes and creative vegetables. Indulge the senses.

TWO POTATO GRATIN

*A classic old-fashioned comfort dish, potato gratin is a hearty addition to any winter meal,
and is a generous full moon food.*

3 sweet potatoes, peeled and sliced
thin

3 russet potatoes, peeled and sliced
thin

1 teaspoon chopped fresh lemon
thyme or thyme

1 teaspoon dried marjoram

Sea salt and freshly ground pepper

6 ounces Gruyère cheese, coarsely
grated

1 cup light sour cream

1 cup half-and-half

Preheat the oven to 375 degrees.

Generously grease a 9 by 12-inch oval gratin dish.

Layer about half of the sweet potato slices in the dish. Season them with ¼ teaspoon lemon thyme, ¼ teaspoon marjoram, sea salt, and pepper. Then layer about half of the russet potatoes, and season with another ¼ teaspoon lemon thyme, ¼ teaspoon marjoram, sea salt, and pepper. Sprinkle 3 ounces of the grated cheese on top. Add another layer of sweet potatoes, season again with ¼ teaspoon lemon thyme, ¼ teaspoon marjoram, sea salt, and pepper, and finish with a layer of russet potatoes.

In a mixing bowl whisk together the sour cream and half-and-half.

Firmly press the potatoes with a large spoon, or spatula, and pour the cream mixture over the sliced potatoes, allowing it to seep in and around the layers, just until it barely covers the top layer. Sprinkle with the remaining lemon thyme and marjoram, and season with sea salt and pepper. Cover the gratin with foil and bake until the potatoes are tender, about 50 to 60 minutes. Remove the foil and sprinkle with the remaining 3 ounces of cheese. Bake for another 15 to 20 minutes, until the potatoes are very tender and the top is nicely browned. Allow the gratin to rest for 10 minutes before serving.

Moonlit Kitchen Tip
Use all Yukon Gold potatoes for a buttery-tasting gratin.

SERVES 6

SUN-KISSED CARROTS BAKED IN FOIL

Sweet and tender carrots infused with the inspiring scent of oranges.
A hint of sunshine amidst the dark of winter—just when we need it most.

1 pound organic carrots, scrubbed, ends trimmed, halved lengthwise, and cut into 3-inch pieces

1 medium red onion, peeled, thinly sliced

Sea salt and freshly ground pepper

1 teaspoon dried cumin or ginger

1 tablespoon orange zest

3 tablespoons olive oil

2 tablespoons honey or real maple syrup

⅔ cup orange juice

Preheat the oven to 425 degrees.

Combine the carrots, onion, sea salt, pepper, cumin, orange zest, and olive oil in a large bowl, and toss to mix.

Cut two large pieces of aluminum foil to make a double thick layer, and center the carrots on the middle of the foil. Cut a piece of foil for the top, match it up, and seal three sides of the foil by folding up the edges and pinching tightly.

Whisk the honey and orange juice together and carefully pour the juice into the open end, then fold the foil and seal it tightly. Bake the carrots for about 40 to 50 minutes, until tender. Check for tenderness by carefully unsealing one end and testing a carrot with a fork. (Use caution when opening the foil packet. Steam will escape!)

SERVES 4

CREAMY GARLIC GRITS

Grits aren't just for breakfast. Creamy clouds of grits make a polenta-like bed
for any of your favorite winter comfort foods. As you stir,
think of something in your life that needs smoothing out.

4 cups water or organic chicken broth

1 cup quick grits (white hominy)

2 garlic cloves, peeled, minced

Dash of fine sea salt and freshly ground pepper

¼ cup (½ stick) butter or margarine

1 cup grated Parmesan or cheddar cheese

In a medium saucepan bring the water or broth to a rapid boil and slowly pour in the grits, stirring constantly with a whisk to keep the grits swirling. (This prevents lumps.) Turn down the heat to low-medium. As the grits begin to thicken, keep stirring, and add the garlic, sea salt, and pepper. If you are using quick grits, they will be cooked in 5 to 7 minutes. (Traditional grits take longer. Follow the directions on the package.) When the grits are soft and creamy, add the butter and stir until melted. Add the cheese and stir until the mixture is well blended. Cover and keep warm until you are ready to serve. If the grits "set," whisk them again to soften.

Moonlit Kitchen Tip

Grits make a wonderful polenta-style side dish. For Southwestern grits, add ½ cup chopped green chilies and substitute Pepper Jack cheese for Parmesan cheese. For a Mediterranean twist, try adding ½ cup chopped oil-packed sun-dried tomatoes, ⅓ cup toasted pine nuts, 1 cup shredded asiago cheese, and 1 tablespoon chopped fresh basil leaves.

Serves 4

LEMON-GINGER GREEN BEANS

A quick and perfect side dish whenever fresh green beans are available.

½ pound fresh green beans, trimmed

2 inches fresh ginger root, peeled and cut into matchsticks

1 tablespoon extra virgin olive oil

1 tablespoon fresh lemon juice

½ teaspoon freshly grated lemon zest

Sea salt and freshly ground pepper

2 tablespoons pine nuts, pecans, or almonds, chopped

Place the beans and ginger in a saucepan filled with 2 quarts of boiling salted water, and quickly cook the beans until they are tender-crisp, 3 to 4 minutes. Drain the gingered beans in a colander.

In a glass measuring cup whisk together the olive oil, lemon juice, lemon zest, sea salt, and pepper. Place the beans in a warmed serving bowl, add the nuts, then the olive oil mixture.

SERVES 4

COCONUT-WHIPPED WINTER SQUASH

Winter squashes whip up beautifully with coconut milk. Add your favorite spices for grounding, and you have an easy winter side dish.

1 large butternut squash, or 2 acorn squash

½ cup (or more) coconut milk, stirred well

2 to 4 tablespoons butter or margarine, cut into pieces

Sea salt and freshly ground pepper

Freshly grated nutmeg

Pinch of cinnamon, allspice, or pumpkin pie spice

Preheat the oven to 375 degrees.

Cut the squash in half and place both pieces cut side down in a baking dish or roasting pan. Pour 1 inch of hot water into the pan to help keep the squash from scorching. Bake the squash for about 45 to 50 minutes, or until it is fork-tender. Remove from the oven and set aside until it is cool enough to handle.

When slightly cooled, scoop out the flesh and either purée it in a food processor or put it in a saucepan and whip it with a sturdy wire whisk. As you purée it, slowly add the coconut milk, pieces of butter, and salt, pepper, nutmeg, and cinnamon to taste. Reheat gently on low heat in a saucepan, if necessary.

Moonlit Kitchen Tip

This recipe also works well with pumpkin or sweet potatoes.

SERVES 4

KARRI ANN'S COLCANNON

The perfect comfort food on a windy March night.
Serve this Irish classic with plenty of melted butter poured into a center "well."

4 large Yukon Gold potatoes

1 tablespoon olive oil plus 3 to 4
     tablespoons olive oil or butter

4 garlic cloves, peeled, minced

1 small head white cabbage, thinly
     sliced

Sea salt and freshly ground pepper

Freshly grated nutmeg

2 to 4 scallions, chopped (white
     parts only)

1 cup milk, heated gently

Scrub the potatoes and cut each one into several pieces. Place them in a saucepan and cover the potatoes with salted water. Over medium-high heat, cook the potatoes, covered, for about 15 minutes, until they are fork tender.

While the potatoes are cooking, gently heat 1 tablespoon olive oil in a nonstick skillet, and add the garlic and cabbage. Season with sea salt, freshly ground pepper, and nutmeg. Stir the cabbage over medium-heat for about 10 minutes, or until the cabbage is very tender (or cover and lower the heat to steam the cabbage, if you prefer).

When the potatoes are fork-tender, drain them in a colander, and pour them into a large warmed pot or mixing bowl. Add the chopped scallions and begin smashing the potatoes with a potato masher, then slowly add the heated milk, 3 to 4 tablespoons olive oil, and the cooked cabbage; mix well. Add sea salt and fresh pepper to taste.

Serving Suggestion

Serve alone as a main dish with sausages on the side, or smothered with the *Balsamic Roasted Chicken and Peppers* (pages 130–131).

Moonlit Kitchen Tip

Try using buttermilk for a tangy change of pace. No buttermilk on hand? Combine your milk with a generous dollop of sour cream or yogurt and blend well.

SERVES 4

ROASTED TOMATOES PROVENCAL

These Provencal-style tomatoes are perfect in the winter months,
when truly ripe and juicy tomatoes are a distant summer memory.

4 to 6 large Italian plum tomatoes
(a.k.a. Roma tomatoes)

Olive oil

½ cup Italian-style seasoned bread
crumbs

4 tablespoons freshly grated
Parmesan cheese

1 tablespoon minced fresh parsley

2 garlic cloves, peeled, minced

Sea salt and freshly ground pepper

Preheat the oven to 325 degrees.

Halve the tomatoes horizontally, gently scoop out the center pulp and seeds, and place them in an oiled cake pan or on a baking sheet, cut sides up. Brush them all over with olive oil and bake them for 20 minutes.

Meanwhile, combine the bread crumbs, Parmesan, parsley, garlic, sea salt, and pepper in a small bowl and toss well. When the tomatoes are roasted, divide the bread crumb topping among the tomatoes.

Preheat the oven to broil.

Drizzle a little extra olive oil over the top of the tomatoes and broil them about 4 inches from the heat for 2 to 3 minutes, or until the topping is sizzling and golden brown.

Moonlit Kitchen Tip

Make your own yummy and magical bread crumbs from leftover stale bread. In a food processor, place torn bread and your favorite fresh herbs from the garden. Process into instant herbed breadcrumbs.

Store extra crumbs in an airtight container.

SERVES 4

PASTA FRITTATA

This quick and savory side dish makes use of leftover spaghetti. Perfect for the waning moon when your intention is to finish up what you started or tie up loose ends.

4 large free-range eggs, beaten

1 cup half-and-half

1 cup shredded asiago, Parmesan, or Pepper Jack cheese

1 (4-ounce) can chopped green chilies, drained

⅓ cup chopped black olives

½ teaspoon chili powder

Sea salt and freshly ground pepper

3 cups leftover cooked spaghetti or linguini

Olive oil cooking spray

1 large tomato, sliced into 4 to 6 slices

2 teaspoons dried marjoram, oregano, or basil

Garnish

Salsa

Sour cream

In a large mixing bowl combine the eggs, half-and-half, cheese, chilies, olives, chili powder, sea salt, and pepper. Add the pasta and mix well.

Heat a large oven-safe nonstick or iron skillet over medium heat, and spray it with cooking spray. (Or make two smaller frittatas if you have an 8-inch skillet.) Pour in the pasta-egg mixture and cook over medium heat for about 5 minutes, until the bottom is set and lightly browned.

Preheat the oven to broil.

Lay the tomato slices on top of the frittata, sprinkle with the marjoram, and place the skillet in the oven. Broil for another 5 minutes, until the eggs are completely set and the top is golden. Remove from the oven and allow it to set for 2 to 5 minutes before cutting into wedges and serving.

Garnish with a spoonful of your favorite salsa and a dollop of sour cream, if desired.

Moonlit Kitchen Tip

Pasta Frittatas can be enjoyed immediately out of the oven, or eaten at room temperature, and make versatile picnic fare. Try your own favorite add-ins, and cook the frittatas ahead of time. Slice into wedges and wrap in foil for an easy take-along food.

SERVES 4 TO 6 AS A SIDE DISH

ASPARAGUS SPEARS IN LEMON VINAIGRETTE

Lovely spring asparagus, thought to lure the most stalwart into the mood of Eros.
A Green Man favorite.

¼ teaspoon freshly grated lemon zest

2 tablespoons fresh lemon juice

3 tablespoons extra virgin olive oil

Dash of balsamic vinegar

Sea salt and freshly ground pepper

1½ pounds thin young asparagus spears, tough bottoms trimmed

Whisk together the lemon zest, lemon juice, olive oil, and vinegar. Season to taste with sea salt and freshly ground pepper, and set aside.

Cook the asparagus spears in a large skillet, over medium-high heat, with just enough salted water to barely cover them. Simmer until the spears are bright green and tender crisp, about 4 to 5 minutes. Do not overcook. Drain any remaining water and arrange the asparagus on a warmed serving plate. Drizzle the vinaigrette all over the asparagus spears and serve immediately.

This recipe may also be enjoyed chilled, as an elegant spring salad.

Moonlit Kitchen Tip

Choose the thinnest, smallest asparagus and keep them chilled, with the bottoms in a glass of water, until cooking time. They are best when very fresh and just barely cooked. Think tender-crisp . . . not soggy!

SERVES 4

LEMONY GARLIC ARTICHOKES

Artichokes are among the thistle family. Serve this quick and easy side dish when someone's been a bit prickly, and you'll see him melt in gratitude before your very eyes.

2 tablespoons olive oil

4 garlic cloves, peeled, minced

1 (10-ounce) package frozen artichoke hearts, thawed on paper towel (or jarred, drained)

⅓ cup fresh lemon juice

3 to 4 tablespoons extra virgin olive oil

Sea salt and freshly ground pepper

Heat 2 tablespoons olive oil in a nonstick saucepan over medium-low heat, add the garlic, and stir for 1 minute. Add the artichokes and cook just until lightly browned. Add the lemon juice and stir. Remove the pan from heat and drizzle with extra virgin olive oil. Season with sea salt and pepper.

Serve the artichokes warm.

SERVES 4

MAPLE BAKED BEANS

The perfect picnic food, easy to toss together on a warm midsummer afternoon.
Let the beans bake slowly in the oven while you work in the herb garden.

1 tablespoon canola or vegetable oil

½ cup red onion, peeled, finely chopped

2 garlic cloves, peeled, minced

1 (15-ounce) can navy beans, drained

1 (15-ounce) can pinto beans, drained

1 (15-ounce) can red kidney beans, drained

1 cup real maple syrup

½ cup catsup

¼ cup light brown sugar

1 tablespoon honey mustard

2 tablespoons Worcestershire sauce

¼ teaspoon ground allspice

1 teaspoon sea salt

Preheat the oven to 325 degrees.

Heat the canola oil on medium heat in an ovenproof Dutch oven or heavy ovenproof pot. Sauté the onion until softened, about 3 minutes. Add the garlic and cook for 1 minute. Remove from heat and combine the beans, maple syrup, catsup, brown sugar, mustard, Worcestershire sauce, allspice, and salt. Cover and bake for 60 to 90 minutes, checking and stirring the beans at least once. If you need to thin the consistency, add a little water.

Moonlit Kitchen Tip

For a change of pace try making an all-white bean casserole by using Great Northern white or cannellini beans, and adding ground cumin, ginger, or curry powder.

SERVES 6

GRILLED HOT POTATOES

Slicing and seasoning baking potatoes adds an elegant touch to this down-home favorite.

4 baking potatoes (no spots or bruises), scrubbed and rubbed well with olive oil

Extra virgin olive oil or melted butter

Sea salt and freshly ground pepper

Fresh chopped dill, mint, or marjoram

Garnish
Sour cream
Fresh snipped chives

Preheat grill to medium-high heat.

Tear off four pieces of aluminum foil (each piece should be large enough to cover the whole potato) and place a potato in the center of each. Using a sharp knife, slice down about ⅔ of the way into each potato, making about 8 cuts across, ¼ inch apart. Generously drizzle olive oil into each of the slices and over the tops of the potatoes. Season with sea salt and pepper. Sprinkle with dill, mint, or marjoram, if desired. Wrap up and close the foil, then place the potatoes on a rack in the hot grill, or to the sides, away from the direct flames. Cover the grill and bake for about 1 hour, or until a fork easily goes into the potatoes.

Open the foil at the top and serve.

Garnish the potatoes with a dollop of sour cream and a dusting of chives, if desired.

Moonlit Kitchen Tip

Make a simple meal out of these yummy potatoes by topping them with a generous spoonful of your favorite baked beans. I always keep a can of good vegetarian baked beans around. By adding real maple syrup, a dash of barbecue sauce, and some favorite spices (cumin, curry, and allspice work well) you can transform canned beans into a delicious convenience food.

SERVES 4

ROASTED CORN ON THE GRILL

Choose tender, fresh local corn the day you expect to roast it.
Farmers like to say, "Get the water boiling before you even pick the corn!"

6 to 8 ears of sweet corn
(depending upon appetites)

Preheat grill to medium-high heat.

Pull back the husks gently to clean out and discard the corn silk. Rewrap the ears in their husks and soak the corn in a pot of cold fresh water for at least 1 hour. Roast the ears on a covered hot grill, preferably on a top rack or off to the sides, for 15 to 20 minutes, turning the ears every so often to keep them from getting too charred. The husks will blacken a bit, giving the corn a wonderful, smoky-roasted flavor.

SERVES 4 TO 6

SANTA FE RICE

Serve this flavorful side dish to honor the harvest . . . any time of year!

2 tablespoons olive oil

1 medium sweet onion, peeled, finely chopped

½ cup finely chopped green or red bell pepper

3 garlic cloves, peeled, minced

½ teaspoon chili powder

½ teaspoon ground cumin

2 cups Texmati or other long-grain rice

½ cup frozen corn kernels

5 cups organic chicken or light vegetable broth

Preheat the oven to 350 degrees.

Heat the olive oil in a 2-quart flameproof casserole dish or saucepan over medium heat and add the onion, pepper, garlic, chili powder, and cumin. Stir well and cover, cooking the onion mixture about 4 minutes, until softened. Add the rice and stir for 3 minutes. Stir in the corn and broth, cover, and bring to a boil.

Bake the rice, covered, in the middle of the oven for 20 minutes, or until the broth is absorbed.

Moonlit Kitchen Tip

For an extra spicy treat, substitute two chopped jalapeno peppers for the sweet peppers and serve with grated cheddar cheese. Add cooked shredded chicken or bite-size pieces of baked tofu and you have a one-pot meal.

SERVES 4 TO 6

SPICED SQUASH AND MAPLE BEANS

Native American culinary gifts include maple syrup, corn, and the classic pairing of squash and beans. Celebrate this month's bounty with this spicy-sweet side dish.

2 tablespoons olive or sunflower oil

1 sweet onion, peeled, diced

4 garlic cloves, peeled, minced

1 teaspoon red pepper flakes

½ teaspoon ginger

¼ teaspoon allspice

1 cup diced yellow squash

1 (15-ounce) can white beans, rinsed and drained

1 (15-ounce) can black beans, rinsed and drained

⅓ cup real maple syrup

⅛ cup chili sauce

2 tablespoons apple cider vinegar

In a heavy skillet heat the oil on medium heat and add the onion, garlic, red pepper flakes, ginger, and allspice. Stir well and cook for 3 minutes, until the onion starts to soften. Add the squash and stir-fry for 5 minutes. Add the beans, maple syrup, chili sauce, and vinegar, mix well, and reduce the heat to low. Cover the pan and simmer the bean mixture for about 15 minutes, stirring occasionally.

Serving Suggestion

This savory side dish is wonderful with chicken, fish, sausages, or any Southwestern-style dish. Spoon over cut baked potatoes and enjoy a rustic supper.

SERVES 4

HARVEST VEGGIE STIR-FRY

Stir up some kitchen magic with your garden's bounty. Fresh herbs make all the difference.

2 tablespoons olive oil

1 onion, peeled, sliced into chunks

2 carrots, julienned

2 yellow squash, cut into half-
moons

1 cup broccoli florets

2 to 3 garlic cloves, peeled, minced

1 tablespoon lemon juice

1 tablespoon freshly chopped basil
or parsley

1 tablespoon freshly chopped mint

Sea salt and freshly ground pepper

Heat the olive oil in a large nonstick skillet or wok over medium-high heat. Add the onion, carrots, squash, broccoli, and garlic, and stir-fry for about 5 minutes. Add the lemon juice and stir for 1 minute. When the vegetables are tender-crisp, stir in the basil and mint. Add salt and pepper to taste.

Serve immediately.

Moonlit Kitchen Tip

Add a dash of magic by using appropriate spices. Toss in pieces of tofu or chicken and you have a quick and savory meal.

SERVES 4

CIDER-ROASTED VEGETABLES

Busy Kitchen Witches love to roast vegetables. This recipe adds the wonderful flavor of apple to its delicious complexity. Add a dash of warm spices to suit your intention.

8 carrots, peeled, sliced at an angle

2 large parsnips, peeled, cut into pieces

½ head cauliflower, cored, cut into pieces

1 large sweet onion, peeled, sliced in chunks

6 to 8 garlic cloves, peeled

2 tablespoons apple cider vinegar

⅓ cup apple cider or apple juice

1 tablespoon light brown sugar

Sea salt and freshly ground pepper

Preheat the oven to 375 degrees.

Combine the carrots, parsnips, cauliflower, onion, and garlic in a roasting pan or large clay baking dish.

In a glass measuring cup whisk together the cider vinegar, apple cider, and brown sugar.

Pour the cider sauce over the vegetables and stir to coat evenly. Season with sea salt and pepper to taste. Roast the vegetables uncovered for about 20 minutes, then stir them with a wooden spoon. Continue roasting until the vegetables are tender but not overdone, another 10 to 15 minutes.

Moonlit Kitchen Tip

Toss together your own combination of vegetables. Remember that dense vegetables (like carrots) take longer to roast than softer veggies (like zucchini). To compensate, cut carrots, parsnips, potato wedges, and onions into thinner pieces, and cut zucchini, summer squash, and mushrooms slightly thicker. Broccoli florets, cauliflower pieces, chunks of fall squashes, and baby red potatoes are all wonderful for roasting. Experiment and have fun!

SERVES 4 TO 6

CINNAMON APPLESAUCE

There's nothing like homemade applesauce to fill the kitchen
with the coziest scents of fall: apples and cinnamon.

3 pounds apples (such as Gala or
Golden Delicious)

1 cup water

⅓ cup light brown sugar, packed

Pinch of sea salt

3 tablespoons fresh lemon juice

1 teaspoon ground cinnamon

Dash of grated fresh nutmeg

Peel and core the apples, and cut into bite-size pieces.

In a heavy, medium saucepan, combine the apples with 1 cup water, brown sugar, and a pinch of sea salt. Bring to a boil, stir, and reduce the heat. Cover the pan and simmer the apples until they are very tender, about 20 to 25 minutes. Remove the cover and continue to simmer until almost all of the liquid in the saucepan has been reduced, about 5 to 6 minutes. Remove the pan from the heat. Add the lemon juice, cinnamon, and nutmeg, and stir. Allow the apples to cool for 30 minutes. Using a potato masher, smash the apples until you have a sauce that's coarse and chunky. If you prefer a smoother sauce, process the apples in a food processor rather than smashing by hand.

This sauce is most flavorful served at room temperature, but you may also chill it, covered, in the refrigerator and serve it cold, if you prefer. Applesauce will keep well for about 3 days. It's best when eaten right away, however.

SERVES 4 TO 6

SESAME-CRUSTED SWEET POTATO WEDGES

Simple potatoes become a slightly crunchy treat with a savory sesame crust.

1½ pounds sweet potatoes, scrubbed, cut into slender wedges

2 tablespoons olive oil

1 tablespoon apple cider vinegar

Sea salt and freshly ground pepper

2 tablespoons toasted sesame seeds

Parboil the potatoes in a pot of boiling water for 3 minutes. Drain well.

Heat the olive oil over medium-high heat and add the sweet potatoes. Stir gently for about 10 minutes. Slowly add the vinegar, and season with sea salt and freshly ground pepper to taste. Continue to cook until the wedges are nicely browned and tender inside. Add the toasted sesame seeds and stir to coat the potatoes well.

Serve immediately.

Moonlit Kitchen Tip

For a change of pace, add herbs such as rosemary, marjoram, lemon thyme, or dill. Add a touch of the fire element by using ground ginger, curry, or cumin.

SERVES 4

BRAISED CABBAGE AND APPLES

Comforting and slightly sweet, this savory cabbage dish is perfect fare for the waning moon.

2 tablespoons olive oil

1 medium onion, peeled, thinly
    sliced

2 tablespoons light brown sugar

1 large head red cabbage, cored,
    thinly sliced

2 tart apples, cored, peeled, diced

½ cup apple cider

2 tablespoons apple cider vinegar

½ teaspoon caraway seeds

½ teaspoons red pepper flakes

Sea salt and freshly ground pepper

Heat the olive oil in a large pan over medium-high heat. Add the onion and sauté until it begins to soften, about 5 minutes. Add the brown sugar and stir well, until the onion caramelizes, about 10 minutes. Add the cabbage and sauté until it wilts, stirring frequently, for about 6 minutes. Add the apples and apple cider. Reduce the heat to medium, cover, and cook until the cabbage and apples are tender, stirring occasionally, for about 5 to 7 minutes. Uncover and add the vinegar, caraway seeds, and red pepper flakes. Stir well and continue to simmer until almost all the liquid evaporates, about 3 minutes. Season with sea salt and freshly ground pepper to taste.

SERVES 4

DILL SMASHED POTATOES

*Being born Irish and Scottish gives me the perfect excuse to cook potatoes
whenever possible. It's a good thing they're so good for us—especially in the darker months,
when they boost serotonin levels.*

1 pound Yukon Gold potatoes,
    peeled, cut into chunks

2 to 4 tablespoons olive oil or
    butter

½ to ¾ cup buttermilk, or sour
    cream thinned with a little milk

1 tablespoon fresh dill, chopped

Sea salt and freshly ground pepper

Garnish
Dill sprig

Place the potatoes into a large pot and cover them with cold, salted water. Bring the water to a boil, and cook the potatoes until they are fork-tender, about 15 to 20 minutes. Drain the potatoes and gently smash them with a masher or large fork (smash them lightly; overbeating potatoes can make them gluey). Add the olive oil, buttermilk, dill, sea salt, and pepper. Keep them warm by covering them until serving.

Add a dill sprig to each serving for garnish.

Moonlit Kitchen Tip

It may be obvious that I prefer to use the versatile Yukon Gold in most of my potato recipes, but Idaho will also make good smashed potatoes. For a change of pace try adding different flavors and herbs to your smashing: roasted garlic, caraway, chives, fresh parsley, rosemary, and even mint!

SERVES 4

WARMED SPINACH IN WALNUT OIL

The trick to cooking spinach is to wilt it briefly rather than to boil it,
then toss it in fragrant oil with sensuous seasonings.

1 to 2 bunches fresh spinach,
   washed carefully, stemmed

Sea salt and freshly ground pepper

⅓ cup walnut or sesame oil

1 tablespoon balsamic vinegar

⅔ cup walnut or pecan pieces

Heat a large open pan on medium-low heat, and place the wet spinach into it, seasoning with sea salt and ground pepper; allow the leaves to steam and wilt from the heat and moisture, about 1 to 2 minutes.

Remove the pan from the heat and pour the walnut oil, balsamic vinegar, and walnuts on the wilted spinach. Lightly toss to coat the leaves.

Serve immediately.

SERVES 4

MAPLE-PECAN ROASTED SQUASH

Another food gift from the Native Americans, maple syrup is made from the sap of sugar maple trees. By boiling the sap to refine and concentrate the flavor, we enjoy the syrup as a natural sweetener, a gift from Mother Earth herself.

2 medium-sized acorn squash, halved crosswise and seeded

Sea salt and freshly ground pepper

¼ cup butter, melted

½ cup pure maple syrup

¼ teaspoon ground allspice, or to taste

2 tablespoons chopped pecans

1 tablespoon currants or golden raisins

Garnish
Chopped pecans

Preheat the oven to 400 degrees.

Brush each squash half lightly with olive oil, season with sea salt and pepper to taste, and arrange them, cut sides down, in a large baking pan. Add about ½ inch of water to the pan to keep the squash from scorching. Bake for 30 minutes.

In the meantime, combine the butter, maple syrup, allspice, pecans, currants, and a pinch of sea salt in a small saucepan and gently heat on low, stirring occasionally.

Remove the squash from the oven, and turn them over, cut sides up. Brush each generously with some of the maple syrup liquid. Spoon some pecans and currants from the mixture into each center well, and return the squash to the oven. Roast the squash for another 20 minutes, brushing the remaining maple syrup mixture on each half once or twice. You may need to add more water to the pan to keep the squash from scorching.

When the squash is very tender, remove from the oven and serve.

Season with sea salt and freshly ground pepper to taste, and garnish with chopped pecans.

SERVES 4

GARLICKY SCALLOPED POTATOES

*Satisfy your moon lover with this classic moon food . . . buttery Yukon potatoes
baked to perfection in a creamy garlicky sauce.*

1 cup heavy cream or half-and-half

¾ cup organic chicken or vegetable
broth

4 to 6 garlic cloves, peeled, minced

1 teaspoon dill or thyme

1 teaspoon sea salt

Freshly ground black pepper

4 ounces chèvre, crumbled, or
freshly grated Parmesan cheese

2 pounds Yukon Gold potatoes,
scrubbed and sliced thinly

⅓ grated Parmesan or cheddar
cheese

Garnish
Freshly chopped parsley or dill

Preheat the oven to 350 degrees.

Oil a 9 by 12-inch oval gratin dish or square baking dish.

In a heavy saucepan combine the cream, broth, garlic, dill, sea salt, and pepper, and heat until the mixture gently simmers. Add the chèvre and whisk until smooth. Remove from the heat.

In the oiled dish, layer the potato slices, one layer at a time, pouring some of the cream over each layer, until the dish is full. Top with the Parmesan cheese and cover loosely with foil. Place the dish on a baking sheet (to catch drips) and bake in the center of the oven for 30 minutes. Remove the foil and continue baking for another 30 minutes, or until the potatoes are golden brown.

Sprinkle with freshly chopped parsley or dill for garnish.

Moonlit Kitchen Tip
To make this a vegan recipe, use soy cream, vegetable broth, and soy cheese.

SERVES 6

Sensuous Salads

*F*reshly picked herbs and crisp greens are nature's tonic, stimulating the body and refreshing the spirit. During warm weather moons, chilled tender salads perk up a dulled appetite and help keep us cool as a cucumber. When the temperature falls, nurture your body with warmed greens lightly tossed in herbed oil and a touch of garlic. Add seasonal fruits, toasted nuts, or shredded cheeses. Greens work their magic year round.

LEMONY CHICKEN CAESAR SALAD

This is a family favorite, and a goddess-send for those nights when you're too tired to cook.
Serve it with a rustic loaf of bread and chilled glasses of Chardonnay.
Every goddess deserves a night off now and then.

1 lemon-pepper roasted chicken from your favorite deli

1 garlic clove, peeled, halved

1 large head romaine lettuce, washed, cored

Juice of 1 fresh lemon

Sea salt and freshly grated black pepper

⅔ cup Caesar dressing

1 cup freshly grated Parmesan cheese

1 cup crispy seasoned croutons

Remove the chicken from the bones, tear it into bite-size pieces, and set aside.

Rub the garlic halves all over the inside of a large salad bowl and discard. Tear the romaine lettuce into pieces, toss into the salad bowl, and add the chicken. Sprinkle with lemon juice, season with sea salt and freshly grated pepper, and pour on the dressing. Toss well. Add the grated cheese and croutons, and toss again.

Serve immediately.

SERVES 4

SPRING GREENS WITH
ASPARAGUS TIPS AND ORANGES

Awaken the Green Man and celebrate the sensuous season with a salad infused with fresh
citrus flavors. Asparagus spears are believed to be an aphrodisiac.

¾ cup orange juice

3 tablespoons balsamic vinegar

1 tablespoon orange zest

2 tablespoons fresh, finely chopped
  basil

½ cup extra virgin olive oil

Sea salt and freshly ground pepper

12 baby asparagus spears

½ Bermuda onion, peeled, sliced
  very thin

2 oranges, peeled, pith removed,
  segmented

6 cups mixed mesclun and herbal
  greens

In a small bowl whisk together the orange juice, balsamic vinegar, orange zest, and chopped basil. Gradually add the olive oil and whisk, then season to taste with sea salt and freshly ground pepper.

Steam the asparagus spears for 2 to 3 minutes, then plunge them into ice water. Drain well. Place the asparagus, onion, and oranges in a bowl, then cover with the salad dressing and allow to marinate for 15 to 30 minutes.

When ready to serve, combine the greens with the prepared mixture. Toss well to mix.

Serve immediately, and offer freshly ground pepper.

Moonlit Kitchen Tip

Many produce sections now carry organically grown mesclun salad mix. Look for an organic mix of herb greens as well. Herbs and bitter greens make a wonderful salad base for spring.

Serves 4 to 6

HERBED FRUIT SALAD

*Celebrate your own summer of love with the Goddess' favored fruits tossed in fragrant herbs
and natural juice. Perfect picnic food for a tryst beneath the shade of an oak tree.*

2 cups white grape juice

1 pint fresh ripe strawberries,
    stemmed, quartered

1 ripe cantaloupe, seeded, cut into
    chunks

1 cup green seedless grapes

1 cup fresh blueberries

1 kiwi fruit, skinned, sliced

1 tablespoon fresh mint, chopped

1 tablespoon fresh lemon balm or
    pineapple mint, chopped

Dash of granulated sugar

Garnish
Fresh mint sprigs

Pour the grape juice into a large bowl and add the fruit,
mint, lemon balm, and a dash of granulated sugar to
taste. Gently mix.

Cover and chill for 2 hours before serving.
Garnish with fresh mint sprigs.

Moonlit Kitchen Tip
Add a touch of elegance to your summer table and
serve this fruit salad in fancy wine or parfait glasses,
topped with fresh mint or lemon balm leaves.

SERVES 6

SUMMER TOMATO SALAD WITH FRESH BASIL

*Tomatoes are the favored fruit of the Love Goddess herself. Ripe summer-fresh tomatoes
paired with basil make a simple salad that is, in a word, sublime.*

6 to 8 small to medium assorted,
   ripened tomatoes in every shape,
   size, and color

1 bunch fresh basil, washed and
   stemmed

Sea salt and freshly cracked pepper

¼ cup extra virgin olive oil

¼ cup balsamic vinegar

1 tablespoon minced shallots

1 garlic clove, peeled, minced

2 teaspoons light brown sugar

Choose an assortment of ripened organic tomatoes at
your local farmer's market: fat and juicy, small and
sweet, yellow and red. Plan on at least 2 tomatoes per
person.

Slice the tomatoes and arrange them on a chilled
platter. Sprinkle the basil on top of the tomatoes.
Lightly season with salt and pepper.

In a small bowl whisk together the olive oil, vinegar,
shallots, garlic, and brown sugar to make a vinaigrette.

Pour the vinaigrette over the tomatoes and basil and
keep cool, away from heat . . . but do *not* refrigerate!

Moonlit Kitchen Tip
Tomatoes will lose their sweet texture if you refrigerate them, so resist. Keep them in a cool spot in your
kitchen if they are ripe. If they need some coaxing to
ripen fully, place them on a sunny windowsill.

Serves 4

CANTALOUPE SALAD WITH COCONUT–SOUR CREAM DRESSING

True goddess love food! This light and cooling fruit salad
makes a refreshing side dish for spicy fare.

1 ripe cantaloupe

⅓ cup light sour cream

2 tablespoons coconut milk plus
   more to thin (if necessary)

1 teaspoon pure vanilla extract

1 tablespoon fresh lime juice

1 teaspoon light brown sugar

Garnish

Grated sweetened coconut

Fresh mint sprigs

Cut and seed the cantaloupe, slice it into bite-size pieces, and place the pieces in a salad bowl.

Whisk together the sour cream, coconut milk, vanilla, lime juice, and brown sugar until mixture is smooth and fluid. Thin with more coconut milk if necessary. Pour the dressing over the cantaloupe and mix gently. Cover and chill for 1 hour.

Serve this melon salad in pretty glass bowls or parfait glasses, and garnish each salad with a sprinkle of grated coconut and a mint sprig.

SERVES 4

GREENS WITH GOAT CHEESE, PEARS, AND TOASTED WALNUTS

This is my favorite salad, especially when pears are in season.

1 cup walnuts, chopped

2 ripe pears

Juice of ½ lemon

2 cups mesclun salad mix or favorite greens

⅓ cup of your favorite balsamic vinaigrette

8 ounces chèvre

Freshly grated black pepper

Preheat the oven to 350 degrees.

Scatter the walnuts onto a baking sheet and lightly toast them in the oven for about 3 to 4 minutes. Observe them carefully to make sure they don't burn. Remove them from the oven and set aside.

Peel, core, and slice the pears; place them in a bowl. Sprinkle the pears with lemon juice and toss well to keep them from discoloring.

Place the salad greens in a bowl and lightly toss with the vinaigrette. Divide the greens among four salad plates. Divide and arrange the pear slices on each plate, in a fan shape. Sprinkle each serving with the chèvre and toasted walnuts. Finish with freshly grated black pepper.

SERVES 4

GRAPEFRUIT AND SPINACH SALAD

*A refreshing and bright accompaniment to earthy roasted dinners
and creamy, cheesy pasta dishes.*

½ cup virgin olive oil

1 garlic clove, peeled, minced

2 teaspoons prepared Dijon
mustard

4 tablespoons sherry or red wine
vinegar

1 teaspoon fennel seeds, crushed

Sea salt and freshly ground pepper

2 pink or red grapefruits

4 cups baby spinach leaves

Garnish
⅛ cup chopped almonds

Combine the olive oil, garlic, mustard, sherry, and fennel seeds in a glass measuring cup and whisk until blended. Season with sea salt and freshly ground pepper.

Peel and remove the white pith from the grapefruits, and pull apart the segments. Combine the grapefruit segments with the dressing and set aside for 20 minutes to 1 hour.

Wash and dry the spinach leaves and place them in a large salad bowl. Add the grapefruit and dressing and toss well to coat.

Sprinkle the almonds on top just before serving. Season with sea salt and freshly ground pepper, if desired.

SERVES 6

CAPE COD TUNA SALAD

I fashioned this simple salad as an appetizer spread for water crackers, but it makes
a delightfully different stuffing for fresh pita bread sandwiches as well.

2 (6-ounce) cans solid white
   albacore tuna, drained well

2 tablespoons red onion, peeled,
   finely diced

⅓ cup finely diced celery

3 to 4 tablespoons mayonnaise

2 tablespoons dried sweetened
   cranberries

½ teaspoon curry powder

Dash of cayenne pepper

Sea salt and freshly ground pepper

2 tablespoons toasted pine nuts or
   slivered almonds

Flake the drained tuna in a mixing bowl and add the onion, celery, mayonnaise, cranberries, curry powder, cayenne, sea salt, and pepper. Mix well. Cover and chill for at least 1 hour. When you are ready to serve, add the toasted nuts, then mix.

Moonlit Kitchen Tip
Tuna is now available in vacuum-packed pouches. Try it. The texture and flavor is superior to canned tuna.

SERVES 4

Sweet Endings

*E*ach moon brings us its lessons and delights; each season, its distinct pleasures. Life offers us the bitter and the sweet. Celebrate your life and passions with a delectable treat. From the rich dark magic of chocolate to the creamy comfort of vanilla, from gingery pineapple to heavenly coconut, here are fifteen tempting sweets to satisfy your cravings. Share them with someone you love.

CHOCOLATE MINT BROWNIES

Mint-kissed chocolate, a favorite goddess combination,
makes these brownies perfect love food during any moon.

½ cup unsweetened cocoa

1½ cups granulated sugar

½ cup (1 stick) unsalted butter,
    melted, or ½ cup vegetable oil

3 large free-range eggs, beaten

1 teaspoon pure vanilla extract

½ teaspoon peppermint extract

¾ cup unbleached all-purpose flour

½ teaspoon fine sea salt

¾ cup semisweet chocolate chips or
    mint chips

Peppermint Frosting

1 cup sifted confectioners' sugar

2 tablespoons unsalted butter, room
    temperature

1 tablespoon milk

½ teaspoon peppermint extract

Drops of green food coloring
    (optional)

Garnish

Fresh mint leaves

Preheat the oven to 350 degrees.

Grease and flour an 8-inch square baking pan, tapping out excess flour.

Combine the cocoa with the granulated sugar in a mixing bowl, and beat in the melted butter until blended. Add the eggs, and the vanilla and peppermint extracts, and beat until mixture is smooth and glossy. Add the flour, salt, and chocolate chips, and stir just until moistened. Spread the batter in the pan and bake in the center of the oven for about 25 to 30 minutes, until the brownies are dry on top and firm to the touch. Cool the brownies in the pan, on a rack, and make the *Peppermint Frosting*.

Spread the frosting over cooled brownies, and chill until set, about 1 hour. Cut the brownies into squares and store in an airtight container until serving. Keep the brownies chilled for a rich, dense texture. When serving, garnish with fresh mint leaves, if desired.

Peppermint Frosting

In a mixing bowl, beat the confectioners' sugar, butter, milk, and peppermint extract until creamy. Add green food coloring, if desired.

MAKES 16 2-INCH BROWNIES

BAKED CROISSANT PUDDING

A heavenly dessert in honor of Brigid, the bride at Imbolc.
Using day-old croissants in place of bread adds an elegance to an old-fashioned classic.

4 large croissants, day-old

½ cup golden raisins or chopped dried apricots

2 cups whole milk

1 cup light cream or half-and-half

4 large free-range eggs, slightly beaten

¾ cup light brown sugar

¼ teaspoon fine sea salt

1 teaspoon pure vanilla extract

Dash of freshly grated nutmeg

Preheat the oven to 350 degrees.

Butter or grease a 2-quart glass baking dish.

Slice the croissants into 1-inch pieces and press them down to line the bottom and sides of the dish. Sprinkle the raisins on top of the croissants.

In a mixing bowl combine the milk, light cream, eggs, brown sugar, sea salt, vanilla, and nutmeg. Beat for 2 minutes, until light and frothy. Pour the pudding mixture over the croissants and press with a flat spoon to allow the liquid to thoroughly soak into the croissants. Cover with foil and set aside. Let stand for 20 minutes.

Set the pudding into a larger roasting pan filled with 2 inches of hot water, and carefully place the pan into the center of the oven. Bake for 30 minutes. Remove the foil and bake for another 20 minutes, until the pudding is set, golden brown, and a bit crusty. Carefully remove the roasting pan from the oven and move the pudding dish from the water bath to a cooling rack. Allow the pudding to rest before cutting and serving.

Serve slightly warm, or cover and chill.

SERVES 6

GINGER-FROSTED PINEAPPLE CAKE

The ease in which this yummy dessert is put together will be between you,
me, and the Goddess.

2 large free-range eggs

1 (20-ounce) can crushed pineapple,
  with juice

2 cups unbleached all-purpose flour

1 cup granulated sugar

1 cup light brown sugar

2 teaspoons baking soda

1 cup chopped walnuts or pecans

Gingered Cream Cheese Frosting

1 (8-ounce) package of Neufchâtel
  or cream cheese

¼ cup (½ stick) butter or
  margarine, softened

1 teaspoon pure vanilla extract

2 to 3 cups confectioners' sugar

¼ teaspoon ground ginger

4 to 5 pieces candied ginger,
  chopped

Garnish

Chopped walnuts or pecans

Preheat the oven to 350 degrees.

Grease a 13 by 9-inch baking pan.

In a large mixing bowl beat the eggs with a fork until they are light and fluffy. Add the crushed pineapple, undrained, and mix well by hand. Add the flour, granulated sugar, brown sugar, and baking soda, and gently beat with a fork. Do not overbeat. Fold in the chopped nuts. Spoon the batter into the baking pan. Bake for 45 minutes, or until a toothpick inserted into the center emerges clean. Let the cake cool in the pan, and make the *Gingered Cream Cheese Frosting*.

Frost the cooled cake and sprinkle with the extra chopped nuts, if desired. This cake keeps well in the refrigerator, covered.

Gingered Cream Cheese Frosting

In a mixing bowl beat the cheese, butter, and vanilla until smooth. Gradually add the confectioners' sugar, one cup at a time, until you achieve the desired consistency. Add the ground ginger, and beat until mixture is smooth and creamy. Add the candied ginger by hand and stir well.

Serves 8 to 10

LEMON PIE WITH RASPBERRY SAUCE

During the heady warm weather moons,
what could be more luscious than the flavors of lemon and raspberry?

5 large free-range eggs

1¼ cup granulated sugar

½ cup (1 stick) melted butter or
  margarine

2 tablespoons cornmeal

4 tablespoons fresh lemon juice

Zest from 1 fresh lemon

⅛ teaspoon fine sea salt

Pinch of grated fresh nutmeg

1 9-inch prepared pie shell, unbaked

Raspberry Sauce

1 pint fresh raspberries, washed just
  before using, drained well

⅓ cup confectioners' sugar

1 teaspoon fresh lemon juice

Garnish

Fresh mint leaves

Lemon balm leaves

Preheat the oven to 325 degrees.

In a mixing bowl beat the eggs with a beater until they are fluffy. Add the granulated sugar, butter, and cornmeal, beating after each addition. Add the lemon juice, lemon zest, sea salt, and fresh nutmeg, and stir. Pour the filling into an unbaked pie shell and bake until firm, about 30 to 35 minutes. The pie is done when a knife inserted into the center emerges clean. Cool on a wire rack, and make the *Raspberry Sauce*.

To serve the pie, slice it into wedges and plate each piece with a drizzle of *Raspberry Sauce* over and around every slice. Garnish with fresh mint or lemon balm leaves.

Raspberry Sauce

Using a blender or food processor, purée the raspberries, confectioners' sugar, and lemon juice. Taste the sauce for desired sweetness, and adjust the sugar or lemon juice as needed. Strain the sauce through a sieve, cover, and refrigerate until you are ready to serve dessert.

Moonlit Kitchen Tip

Frozen raspberries will work as a substitute for fresh berries.

SERVES 8

STRAWBERRY SNOW

This light and lovely dessert is the perfect end to an outdoor grilled supper.
Indulge beneath a moonlit sky with someone you love.

1 quart freshly picked strawberries, washed and stemmed

1 cup superfine granulated sugar

1 (4-ounce) carton pasteurized egg whites

Pinch of salt

1 pint whipping cream, whipped with ½ teaspoon pure vanilla extract

Garnish
Strawberries

Fresh mint sprigs, washed

Process the strawberries roughly in a food processor by pulsing on and off, adding the granulated sugar a little at a time, until you have a purée.

In a separate large bowl beat the egg whites with the salt until the mixture forms stiff peaks. Gently fold the strawberry purée into the egg whites, then softly fold in the whipped cream. Spoon the strawberry snow into six pretty dessert glasses and serve immediately, topped with a whole strawberry and a sprig of mint for garnish. (If you are not serving immediately, do not garnish. Lightly cover each dessert with plastic wrap and keep well chilled in the refrigerator, and garnish just before serving.)

Serving Suggestion
Strawberry Snow is lovely when paired with *Lemon Herb Cookies* (page 190).

SERVES 8

COCONUT CAKE

I cannot guarantee you'll have visions of Tahitian Goddesses,
*but this **Coconut Cake** does taste like a little piece of paradise.*

2½ cups sifted cake flour

2 teaspoons baking powder

¼ teaspoon salt

1 cup (2 sticks) butter or butter-flavored vegetable shortening

1½ cups granulated sugar

3 large free-range eggs (separate the yolks from the eggs)

1 teaspoon coconut or pure vanilla extract

1 cup milk

1 cup shredded sweetened coconut

Preheat the oven to 350 degrees.

Grease and flour 2 9-inch cake pans.

Sift together the flour, baking powder, and salt; set aside.

In a mixing bowl cream the butter and add the granulated sugar gradually, until mixture is light and fluffy. Add the egg yolks and beat well. Add the coconut extract. Add the dry ingredients, alternating with the milk, and beating after each addition. Add the coconut, and stir.

In a small bowl beat the egg whites until they are stiff, then fold them carefully into the cake batter. Pour the batter into the prepared pans, and bake for 25 to 30 minutes, or until a toothpick inserted in the center emerges clean. Allow the cakes to cool for 10 to 15 minutes before turning them out onto a rack. Cool completely before frosting with *Coconut Cream Cheese Frosting.*

Place one cake on a cake plate and spread about ½ cup of frosting over the top surface. Place the other cake on top. Spread the remaining frosting on the top and sides of the cake.

Coconut Cream Cheese Frosting

½ cup (1 stick) butter, softened, or butter-flavored vegetable shortening

2 (8-ounce) packages cream cheese, softened

1 teaspoon coconut or pure vanilla extract

1 tablespoon lemon juice

1 pound confectioners' sugar

½ cup shredded coconut

Garnish

Shredded coconut

Fresh flowers (organic, unsprayed), such as violets, panseys, or marigolds

Coconut Cream Cheese Frosting

Combine the butter, cream cheese, coconut extract, and lemon juice in a mixing bowl. Slowly add the confectioners' sugar as you beat the frosting, until it is smooth, creamy, and spreadable. Add the coconut, and mix gently.

Garnish the frosted cake with a sprinkle of coconut and fresh flowers, if desired.

Moonlit Kitchen Tip

Plate cake slices with swirls of *Raspberry Sauce* (page 186) for added flourish.

SERVES 8 TO 10

LEMON HERB COOKIES

Fresh herbs make delightful and magical additions to many desserts.
Try these lemony cookies infused with an herbal twist.
Substituting minced lavender buds for the lemon thyme creates a lemon-lavender sensation.

1 cup (2 sticks) sweet butter, softened

1 cup granulated sugar

1 cup light brown sugar

2 large free-range eggs, lightly beaten

⅓ cup sour cream

2 tablespoons fresh lemon juice

1 tablespoon lemon zest

1 teaspoon pure vanilla extract

4 cups unbleached all-purpose flour

1 tablespoon baking powder

1 teaspoon baking soda

½ teaspoon fine sea salt

4 teaspoons fresh lemon thyme or lemon balm leaves, finely chopped

Preheat the oven to 350 degrees.

Grease a cookie sheet.

In a large mixing bowl cream the butter, granulated sugar, and brown sugar with an electric beater. Add the eggs, sour cream, lemon juice, and lemon zest, and beat well.

In a separate bowl stir together the flour, baking powder, baking soda, salt, and lemon thyme. Add the dry ingredients to the creamed mixture and beat until mixed.

To make the cookies, drop the dough by spoonfuls, 3 inches apart, on the greased cookie sheet. Flatten slightly with your thumb or a fork. Bake the cookies for 8 to 10 minutes, until they are just starting to brown around the edges. Cool the cookies briefly and, using a spatula, move them to a rack.

When cookies are completely cool, store them in an airtight container.

Moonlit Kitchen Tip

When using herbs in baking, keep in mind that fresh herbs usually have more a subtle flavor. If you are substituting dried herbs, use less than the amount given for fresh herbs. It's always wise to taste test.

MAKES 6 DOZEN COOKIES

RASPBERRY-PEACH COBBLER

Cobblers are old-fashioned desserts that are perfect for today's busy cooks.
They are fresh, fast, and simple to put together.

6 ripe peaches, peeled, halved, and pitted

1 cup fresh raspberries, gently rinsed and patted dry

¾ cup plus 4 tablespoons light brown sugar

1 tablespoon cornstarch

6 tablespoons butter or margarine

2 large free-range eggs

1 teaspoon pure vanilla extract

¾ cup unbleached all-purpose flour

½ teaspoon baking powder

¼ teaspoon salt

Preheat the oven to 350 degrees.

Grease and lightly flour an ovenproof dish (such as an 8-inch oval gratin or an 8-inch baking pan).

Slice the peaches into 1-inch wedges and gently combine them with the raspberries, 2 tablespoons of brown sugar, and cornstarch.

In a separate mixing bowl beat together the butter, ¾ cup brown sugar, eggs, and vanilla until light and fluffy. Add the flour, baking powder, and salt, and mix well. Pour the batter over the peaches, and sprinkle the remaining 2 tablespoons of brown sugar over the top. Bake in the oven for 40 to 45 minutes.

Serving Suggestion

Serve the cobbler warm, with a scoop of vanilla ice cream or frozen yogurt.

Moonlit Kitchen Tip

If you don't have raspberries on hand, try substituting ½ cup of chopped candied ginger for the raspberries. This will give the cobbler a spicy-peachy twist.

SERVES 8

FROZEN MARGARITA PIE

The witches in the film Practical Magic *liked to conjure up pitchers of midnight margaritas. Whip up your own magic with this tart and tasty confection!*

4 cups vanilla ice cream,
  softened

1 (6-ounce) can frozen limeade
  concentrate, thawed

¼ cup tequila

2 tablespoons Triple Sec or
  Cointreau

1 prepared graham cracker or
  cookie piecrust

Garnish

Whipped cream

Fresh lime slices or mint leaves

Place a large metal bowl (or pan) in the freezer for 30 minutes.

Gather the ingredients and quickly combine the ice cream, limeade, tequila, and Triple Sec in the chilled bowl, stir or whip to blend, and immediately return the bowl to the freezer for 30 minutes.

Spoon the partially frozen ice cream mixture into a prepared graham cracker piecrust, and smooth the top surface evenly. Cover with plastic wrap and freeze the pie for at least 4 hours.

Garnish each slice topped with a spoonful of fresh whipped cream and a thin slice of lime or a mint leaf.

SERVES 8

CAPE COD APPLE PIE

Here on Cape Cod we add cranberries to many traditional dishes.
Their tangy sourness is a perfect counterpoint to sweet desserts.

3 tart apples (such as Granny Smith)

3 Golden Delicious or Macoun apples

½ cup light brown sugar, firmly packed

½ cup granulated sugar

2 tablespoons all-purpose flour or cornstarch

Juice from 1 fresh lemon

1 teaspoon ground cinnamon

¼ teaspoon fresh ground nutmeg

¾ cup dried sweetened cranberries

1 prepared pastry for a 9-inch double crust pie

2 tablespoons butter or margarine, cut into pieces

Milk for brushing pastry

Preheat the oven to 425 degrees.

Peel, core, and slice the apples, then place them in a large bowl. Add the brown sugar, granulated sugar, flour, lemon juice, cinnamon, nutmeg, and cranberries, and toss well, until the apples are evenly coated.

Line the pie dish with a prepared crust, and fill with the apple filling, mounding the apples higher in the center to create a dome shape. Dot the filling with bits of butter. Place the second piecrust on top of the filling, and trim off any excess crust. Moisten the edges of both the top and bottom crusts, and pinch them together to seal. Using your forefinger knuckle, press down into the crust edge, and crimp the crust. Lightly brush the top crust with a little milk or water, if desired. Carefully make three slits into the center of the top crust. Bake the pie for 10 minutes. Turn the heat down to 350 degrees and continue baking for about 45 minutes. Protect the crust edges with strips of foil if they brown too quickly. The pie is done when the crust is golden brown and the apples are tender. Juices should bubble up through the slits, and pop. Set the pie on a rack to cool for at least 30 minutes before slicing and serving.

Serving Suggestion

Serve warm with a slice of cheddar cheese or a scoop of *Nutmeg Ice Cream* (page 196).

SERVES 6 TO 8

PUMPKIN CHEESECAKE

A creamy, delightful cheesecake with a hint of pumpkin flavor.

8 ounces Neufchâtel or cream
    cheese, softened

1 (14-ounce) can sweetened
    condensed milk

1 (14-ounce) can pumpkin purée

2 large free-range eggs, lightly
    beaten

2 teaspoons pumpkin pie spice,
    cinnamon, or allspice

½ teaspoon freshly grated nutmeg

½ teaspoon fine sea salt

1 teaspoon pure vanilla extract

1 prepared graham cracker piecrust

Garnish
Whipped cream
Freshly grated nutmeg

Preheat the oven to 350 degrees.

In a large mixing bowl beat the cheese with an electric mixer at medium speed, until smooth and fluffy. Gradually beat in the sweetened condensed milk until smooth. Add the pumpkin purée, eggs, pumpkin pie spice, nutmeg, sea salt, and vanilla, and beat until smooth. Pour the mixture into the prepared piecrust and bake for 50 to 55 minutes, or until the center is set. Cool the cheesecake in the pan on a wire rack.

When the cheesecake is cooled, lightly cover and refrigerate for 2 hours.

Garnish chilled wedges with a dollop of whipped cream and a pinch of freshly grated nutmeg.

SERVES 8

INDIAN PUDDING WITH CRANBERRIES

Try this lovely pairing of two Native American culinary gifts, cornmeal and cranberries.
This soothing, old-fashioned dessert offers warmth and comfort
on nights when the frost fairies etch their icy magic.

2 cups whole milk

3 cups half-and-half

⅓ cup molasses

⅓ cup light brown sugar

⅓ cup granulated sugar

⅓ cup yellow cornmeal

1 teaspoon pure vanilla extract

¾ teaspoon sea salt

1 teaspoon cinnamon

¼ teaspoon nutmeg, freshly grated

⅔ cup sweetened dried cranberries

Garnish
Whipped cream (optional)

Nuts (optional)

Freshly grated nutmeg

Preheat the oven to 300 degrees.

Grease a casserole dish or glass baking dish.

Heat the milk and 2 cups of half-and-half gently in a double boiler until the mixture begins to steam. Whisk in the molasses, brown sugar, granulated sugar, cornmeal, vanilla, sea salt, cinnamon, and nutmeg, stirring constantly until the mixture gently simmers and begins to thicken. Add the cranberries, and stir. Pour the pudding into the greased casserole dish or glass baking dish, and bake for 30 minutes. Add the remaining 1 cup of half-and-half, stir, and let the pudding bake for 30 minutes. Stir again, and continue to bake for another 60 minutes, stirring once more, if you desire.

Garnish with whipped cream topped with nuts and freshly grated nutmeg.

Serving Suggestion
Serve the pudding warm, with a scoop of *Nutmeg Ice Cream* (page 196).

SERVES 8

NUTMEG ICE CREAM

*Enhance your favorite vanilla ice cream with some freshly grated nutmeg
and bring a touch of warming spice into your life!*

1 quart of your favorite natural
    vanilla ice cream, softened
Whole fresh nutmeg

Scoop the softened ice cream into a mixing bowl and grate a generous amount of nutmeg on the ice cream; stir, mixing well. Taste test for the right amount of nutmeg flavor. Spoon the ice cream back into the container and refreeze.

Nutmeg Ice Cream makes a perfect addition to baked autumn desserts—from pumpkin pie and apple crisp to *Indian Pudding with Cranberries* (page 195).

MAKES 1 QUART

FLOURLESS DARK NIGHT CAKE

For those who prefer their chocolate as intense as possible,
not even diluted with flour, here is the cake for you!

12 ounces bittersweet chocolate, chopped, or semisweet morsels

¾ cup (1½ sticks) unsalted butter, cut into pieces

2 teaspoons pure vanilla extract

7 large free-range eggs

1 cup light brown sugar

Garnish
Confectioners' sugar

Raspberries or mint leaves

Preheat the oven to 350 degrees.

Grease a 9-inch springform pan. Line the bottom of the pan with parchment paper, then butter the paper. Wrap the outside of the pan with foil.

Place the chocolate, butter, and vanilla in a heavy saucepan over low heat and stir until the chocolate is melted and smooth. Remove from the heat and allow mixture to cool to lukewarm. Stir it often to keep it smooth.

Using an electric mixer, beat the eggs and brown sugar in a large mixing bowl until the mixture is thick and flows in ribbons, about 6 minutes. Fold about one-half of the egg and brown sugar mixture into the lukewarm chocolate mixture. Fold in the remaining portion of the mixture, and gently blend. Pour the batter into the prepared pan and bake for about 50 to 55 minutes. A toothpick inserted into the cake's center will emerge with a few moist crumbs when done. The top should be a bit puffy, perhaps cracked. Cool the cake in the pan, on a wire rack. If the cake is uneven, gently press down on the top while it is cooling to even it off. Loosen the cake from the edges of the pan with a small spatula. Release the spring clasp. You may serve it right-side up or invert it onto a 9-inch serving plate and peel off the parchment.

For garnish, dust the cake with confectioners' sugar and a few scattered raspberries or mint leaves, if desired.

SERVES 10 TO 12

BLUE MOON BERRY CRISP

If the blue moon happens to fall during a warm month when blueberries are fresh, you're in luck. To plan ahead for cold weather blue moons, freeze summer blueberries in zip-lock bags.

6 cups blueberries, fresh or frozen, washed (or thawed)

½ cup plus 2 tablespoons all-purpose flour

⅓ cup granulated sugar

½ cup shelled natural pistachios or almonds, finely chopped

2 teaspoons cinnamon

1 cup light brown sugar, firmly packed

½ teaspoon salt

¾ cup (1½ sticks) cold butter or margarine, cut into pieces

Preheat the oven to 350 degrees.

Grease a 2-quart casserole dish.

In a large mixing bowl combine the blueberries with 2 tablespoons flour and the granulated sugar; toss well and set aside.

In a separate bowl combine the remaining ½ cup flour, and the pistachios, cinnamon, brown sugar, and salt; mix well. Add the pieces of butter to the mixture. Mix by rubbing the butter and the dry ingredients between your palms, crumbling the mixture until it resembles a coarse meal.

Pour the blueberry mixture into the baking dish and smooth the pistachio-crumb mixture on top of the berries, covering them completely. Bake for 45 minutes, until the topping is nicely browned and the berries are bubbling.

Serving Suggestion
Serve while still slightly warm, with a generous scoop of natural vanilla ice cream or *Nutmeg Ice Cream* (page 196).

SERVES 6 TO 8

AFTERWORD

In a material world that clamors for our attention, our energy, and our paycheck, cooking, for many, has become a bore, a duty, or simply routine. Convenience and speed have taken priority over the old-fashioned notion of nurturing body and soul. Gathering together for a meal and conversation has been replaced with drive-throughs and the shopping mall food court. What is missing in this lure of convenience and food to-go? In two words: *the sacred*. The sense of connection and nurture. The essence of the Goddess.

Honoring our body's intuition by paying attention to its needs and taking the time to become conscious of our appetites honors the spark of the divine within us. Using the thirteen moons as our archetypal guide we surrender our ego and savor the lessons of each season. This very surrender liberates our intuition. Magic is not about changing the will of others or altering circumstances to suit our own desires. True magic is about the archetypal journey toward wholeness, toward authenticity. It is an alchemical journey, and our vessel is the very body we inhabit.

It is my sincere hope that *Cooking By Moonlight* has inspired you to tune in to the subtle changes of each season and rediscover the ancient wisdom of the Goddess in her array of fruits, herbs, vegetables, grains, and spices. Making magic in the kitchen is an art as old as fire itself. Culinary craft is a worthy pursuit. Now, more than ever, it is a skill that needs to be hailed again. My hope is that these recipes and offerings rekindle your desire to stir up your own alchemy in the kitchen and inspire you to share the magic with someone you love. Bright, delicious blessings!

APPENDIX A

Resources & Pantry Supplies

Atlantic Spice Company
P.O. Box 205
Truro MA 02652
1-800-316-7965
website: http://www.atlanticspice.com

Bob's Red Mill Natural Foods
Natural Stone Ground Whole Grain
5209 SE International Way
Milwaukie OR 97222
1-800-349-2173
website: http://www.bobsredmill.com

Cape Cod Lavender Farm
P.O. Box 611
Harwich MA 02645
508-432-8397
website: http://www.capecodlavenderfarm.com

The Gluten Free Pantry
P.O. Box 840
Glastonbury CT 06033
1-860-633-3826
website: http://www.glutenfreepantry.com

Great Cape Herbs
P.O. Box 1206
Brewster MA 02631
1-800-427-7144
website: http://greatcape.com

Hain-Celestial Foods
Natural and Specialty Foods
e-mail: consumeraffairs@hain-celestial.com
website: http://www.hain-celestial.com

Imagine Foods
Organic Soups, Broths, and Natural Foods
1245 San Carlos Avenue
San Carlos CA 94070
1-650-595-6300
website: http://www.imaginefoods.com

Newman's Own
Pasta Sauces, Salad Dressings, Snacks, Organics
website: http://www.newmansown.com

San Francisco Herb Company
250 14th Street
San Francisco CA 94103
1-800-227-4530
website: http://www.sfherb.com

Seeds of Change
Goodness From the Ground Up: Organic Seeds and Organic Foods
P.O. Box 15700
Santa Fe NM 87506
1-888-762-7333
website: http://store.yahoo.com/seedsofchange/ourorfoodpro.html

Thai Kitchen
1919 Market Street
Suite 100
Oakland CA 94607
1-510-268-0209 ext. 103
website: http://www.thaikitchen.com

APPENDIX B

US to UK Translations: Cooking Terms and Ingredients

All-purpose flour: plain flour

Beans, canned: assorted tinned beans, black, pinto, et cetera

Bermuda onion: red or purple skinned sweet onion

Biscuit: scone

Blender: liquidizer

Boboli: premade Italian-style flatbread or pizza shell

Brown sugar: soft brown sugar

Chickpeas: garbanzo or ceci beans

Chicken broth: chicken stock

Chilies: chillis

Cilantro: coriander leaves or Chinese parsley

Cocoa: cocoa powder

Coconut, flaked: desiccated coconut

Cookie: biscuit

Cookie sheet: baking tray

Confectioners' sugar: icing sugar

Corn: maize

Cornbread: bread made with cornmeal

Cornmeal: ground maize

Cornstarch: cornflour

Cream and heavy cream: double cream

Eggplant: aubergine

Extract: essence

Frosting: icing

Golden raisins: sultanas

Graham cracker: digestive biscuit

Great Northern (white) beans: white navy or cannellini

Green beans: French or runner beans

Half-and-half: half cream

Italian blend four cheeses: grated mix of Italian cheeses, hard and soft

Kalamata olives: Greek purple olives

Light cream: single cream

Linguini: pasta noodles in long, flat strands

Mesclun: young rocket, endive, spring greens and herb mix

Mexican vanilla extract: vanilla essence

Minced garlic: finely chopped garlic

Piecrust: pastry case

Plastic wrap: Clingfilm

Polenta: thick maize porridge

Portobello mushroom: large Italian meaty mushroom

Pumpkin pie spice: mixed spice

Preserves: jam

Process: finely chop or liquefy

Parmigiano-Reggiano: Parmesan cheese

Roma tomatoes: Italian plum tomatoes

Romano cheese: hard sheep's milk cheese

Scallions/green onions: spring onions

Shredded cheese: grated cheese

Soy cream: soya cream

Soy milk: soya milk

Spanish onion: large white sweet onion

Sugar: caster sugar

Sun-dried tomatoes, dried: sun-dried tomatoes in oil, drained

Sweet corn: whole kernel corn

Sweet pepper: bell pepper

Texmati rice: long grained white rice or basmati

Vanilla extract: vanilla essence

Vegetable broth: vegetarian stock

Vidalia onion: sweet large yellow onion

Wax paper: greaseproof paper

Yellow pepper: yellow bell pepper, sweet

Yellow Finn potatoes: yellow fleshed potatoes

Yukon Gold potatoes: yellow fleshed potatoes

Zest: grated citrus skin

Zucchini: courgette

APPENDIX C

For volume to weight conversions: http://www.culinarycafe.com/UK_US.html
For liquid and dry measure equivalents: http://www.culinarycafe.com/Liquid.html
For oven temperatures: http://www.samcooks.com/conversion.html

Liquid Measures

1 gallon (4 quarts) = 3.79 l   1 cup (8 oz) = 225 ml
1 quart (2 pints) = 0.95 l   1 tablespoon (½ oz) = 16 ml
1 pint (2 cups) = 450 ml   1 teaspoon (⅓ tablespoon) = 5 ml

Oven Temperatures

225F = 105C   350F = 180C
250F = 120C   375F = 190C
275F = 130C   400F = 200C
300F = 150C   425F = 220C
350F = 150C   450F = 230C
325F = 165C   475F = 245C

Dry Weight Measures

1 ounce = 28.4 g
1 pound = 454 g
1 kg = 2.2 pounds

INDEX